I0891935

GASTON PETIT–

THE KIMONO AND THE CROSS

INTERVIEW WITH AN ARTIST IN JAPAN

GASTON PETIT–

THE KIMONO AND THE CROSS

INTERVIEW WITH AN ARTIST IN JAPAN

BY LINDA GHAN

Signature
EDITIONS

© 2002, Linda Ghan

All rights reserved. No part of this book may be reproduced, stored in a retrieval system or transmitted in any form or by any means without written permission from Signature Editions, except for brief excerpts used in critical reviews.

Book design by Doowah Design.
Cover painting: *Noren VII, The Trapped Eye* by Gaston Petit.

We acknowledge the financial assistance of the Manitoba Arts Council and The Canada Council for the Arts for our publishing program.

Printed and bound in Canada.

National Library of Canada Cataloguing in Publication

Ghan, Linda
Gaston Petit : the kimono and the cross : interview with an artist in Japan / Linda Ghan.

ISBN 0-921833-81-4

1. Petit, Gaston, 1930-. 2. Artists--Canada--Biography. 3. Expatriate artists--Japan--Biography. I. Title.

N6549.P47G46 2002 709'.2 C2002-904513-4

Signature Editions
P.O. Box 206, RPO Corydon, Winnipeg, MB R3M 3S7

CONTENTS

INTRODUCTION

Gaston Petit, a multilingual Quebecer, divides his time between Champlain, Quebec, and Tokyo. He works in sculpture, stained glass, lithography, painting, and church design. Petit's painting and prints have shown all over the world: New Dehli, Paris, London, Montreal, San Francisco... His work can be found in museums and in the private collections of prime ministers and princes.

The essence of Gaston Petit is an enormous curiousity which informs every aspect of his life, from his deep research into his own faith; to travels to the world's major artistic and religious sites; to explorations of the artistic possibilities of glass or paper, the Japanese kimono or the noren... The joy of discovery, to use his own phraseology, seems to overcome discomfort, time, or even pain.

The interviews with Gaston Petit took place over a period of two years: they were jottings from telephone conversations, e-mailed exchanges in French and in English, notes after a service in the Catholic church of Shibuya, or chats with him in his garden in Quebec overlooking the majestic St. Lawrence. The conversations ranged from avant-garde art, to interpretation of sin, to cross-cultural experiences of Canada and Japan. During this period he experienced the first frustrations of serious illness; he no longer works through the night, but has adapted to pacing himself. Nevertheless, taking time out to answer yet another question, he juggled completion of the design of a bronze wall mural (his studio floor completely overtaken by styrofoam forms, eliciting stern injunctions to "Watch where you step!"), visits to Nagasaki to consult with the foundry, designs for a stained glass window, and officiating at church. Through good days and bad, waiting for medical results, recuperating from an operation, I never encountered him less than optimistic. Frustrated, perhaps, angry with himself for being ill, for being slowed, but never depressed.

It was difficult, sometimes, keeping him on track, for as both artist and priest, he is a consummate observer as well as a compassionate listener, and the interviewer often became the interviewee. Because we come from completely different backgrounds (French Catholic: Jewish; old Quebecois roots; prairie immigrant), there were many questions on both sides.

What began as simply an intriguing "project" on a Canadian artist-priest in Japan became an engrossing and enriching experience. A gift. The enthusiasm of Gaston Petit for life's possibilities and for art in all its forms is contagious.

I
CHOCOLATE AND THE CHINESE LAUNDRY

Gaston Petit's personal history gives an entry into the richness of the culture of Quebec. Born in Shawinigan in 1930, Petit's ancestry in Canada goes back to 1656. He grew up an urban child, but summers and Sundays were spent on the family farm. His parents expressed an openness that was unusual for the time, a characteristic manifested in Petit, who went on to embrace the art, language, and culture of Japan.

Gaston Petit focuses almost totally on the present and on the next project. He absorbs life's experiences and moves on. While discussions on art, for instance, needed very little prompting, questions on his early years—his relationship with his vast family, the transition from a teenager involved in skiing and the violin to the cloistered life of a novitiate—had to be specific.

You speak very little about your childhood. The fact that you painted your mother many times suggests a strong emotional bond with her. You never painted your father, however. Was your relationship with your mother stronger, or at least warmer?

Warmer… Perhaps. In those days, the father was a patriarchal figure, the one who earned the daily bread and needed his rest at night. Fathers did not play. They did not do any sports with their children. Children played together. Anyway, my father was not the athletic type.

True. In those days, fathers—everyone's father—were not unlike the salaryman of Japan today, working long hours and on weekends, taking very few holidays. I saw my father a lot only because we lived above his general store, and the store was part of our playground—hide and seek behind the clothes. Otherwise, we wouldn't have seen him—train nights, he was there till 1:00 or 2:00 a.m., for instance. This was much before the modern era of the forty-hour work week in North America.

Yes. And pre-war, there was no question of women working outside the home. Anyway, my mother enjoyed keeping house. So there would be a stronger emotional bond with good reason. I never doubted that my mother would be there; this is one thing that I always remember about her with love. I would come running into the house after school to report on my adventures, and she was waiting with a snack, waiting to listen.

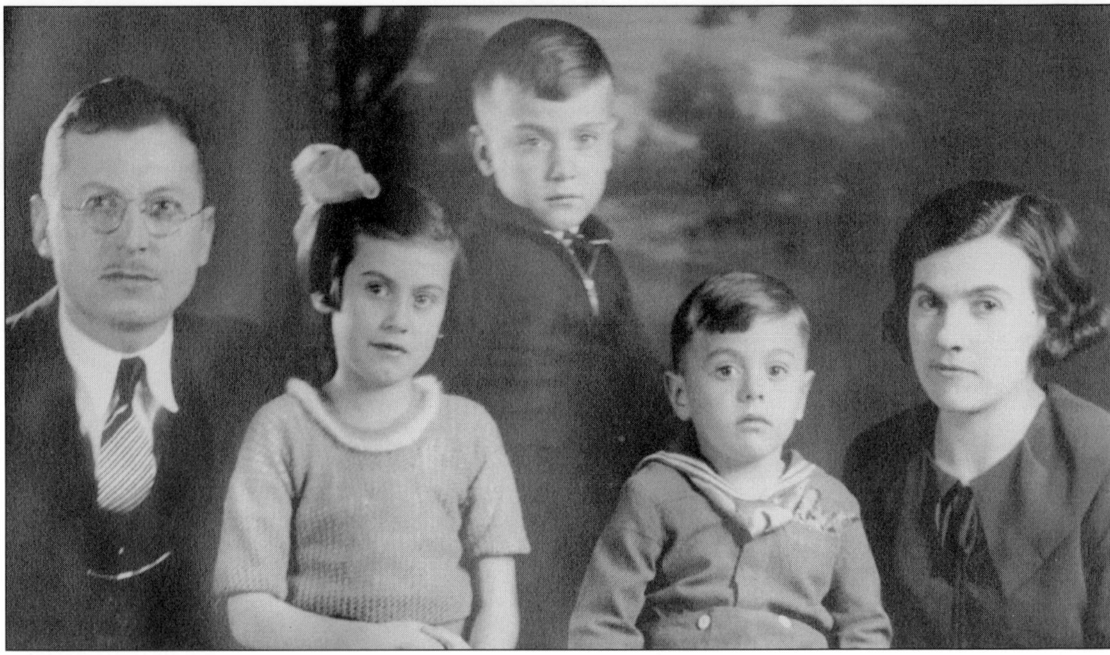

The Petit family: Arthur, Jacqueline, Gilles, Gaston and Antoinette, 1934.

Frank McCourt says in *Angela's Ashes* that a happy childhood is hardly worth mentioning. His was so unhappy. My childhood, even with restrictions of all kinds during the war years, was anything but unhappy.

Your father had an inter-provincial reputation as a salesman, even though he had only a grade eight education. But of course that was not uncommon then, since going on to high school was still a luxury in the twenties and thirties and into the forties. It was more common for the girls to finish high school; the boys often had to quit school to work. I believe your father achieved some notoriety for selling an entire carload of chocolate?

Yes—truly an exploit. The company was astonished. They didn't believe it. They called that night to talk to my father: "Is this correct? It is not an error?" They sent both congratulations and a bonus.

Imagine what it was like for a child to have as his father a famous seller of chocolate. Imagine our visits to the company on Viau Street—to see row after row, shelf after shelf, of candies, cookies and chocolate, in all shapes and colours. As we walked in with our father, one of the workers would hand each of the three of us, Jacqueline, Gilles, and I, a big brown paper bag that we could fill with anything, as much as we wanted.

How old was your father when he had his first job?

I don't really know. My grandfather was a farmer—he died when my father was fourteen. Not all the boys could live off the family farm, and my grandmother had had the foresight to send him to learn a trade. Unfortunately, it was a trade that did not interest him—cheesemaking. I know he went to the United States for at least a year—many of the Québécois went to the US in the winter. The men either went logging in the winter—hard physical labour, hard conditions—or they went to Massachusetts—Mass, as we called it—or Maine, mainly Mass, to work in the large cotton mills. Weaving factories. Women went as well. That's where my grandparents, my mother's parents, met, in fact. They were both working in factories there. They were married in St. Augustine's Church in Lowell, Massachusetts, and my mother's oldest brother was born there. I remember, as a child, family visits to some of my mother's cousins who had remained in the US—I remember being highly amused by the French they were speaking, a very odd mixture of French and English. They had forgotten almost all of their French.

In fact, my Aunt Gracia, who is now ninety-five, still glows when she talks about her handsome husband-to-be as he came courting from the United States, all dressed in white. She was very much in love with her husband all her life. I spent an afternoon with her last summer, and she told me the entire story—I could see that she was reliving the romance by the shine in her eyes.

Is she proud of her nephew the artist, who has paintings hanging in the homes of prime ministers and princes?

She doesn't know. When I go to see her, we speak of other things. She is my aunt, I'm her nephew.

Sorry—we've lost the thread of your father, famous seller of chocolate.

Not exactly; she is the younger sister of my father, famous seller of chocolate.

My father was always a salesman, six different employers in ten years, not unusual at that time… the Carling beer company, a laundry company by the name of Poissant, then the Viau Company, where he earned his fame. This is when we moved finally to Trois-Rivières in 1936. The carload of chocolate also led to an invitation from London, Ontario. The McCormick Company, makers of cookies and candy. They came to offer Papa a job with a raise in wages. A nice promotion, no?

Which he turned down, evidently, since your family remained in Trois-Rivières.

I believe that the family relationships, both with his family and my mother's, and the French culture were more important than the salary and the promotion. I don't know for certain; I don't remember it being discussed. I was too young.

I admire my father a great deal, his openness, his values, his courage and tenacity. He often came home dead tired, but after supper, no matter what, he straightened out his sales accounts, and good weather or bad, went to post a big brown envelope at the train station on Champflour Street. The train to Montreal arrived a little after nine in the evening. The very next morning, very early, the company would retrieve the envelope and could then fill the orders right away. Efficiency was the rule.

He worked hard to draw up these sales reports. With only a grade eight education, it must have been an effort. Often he would ask my mother how to spell one or another word.

So you are your father's son. You have the same focus, the same tenacity. You finish no matter what, too. You put in all-nighters—or used to—to get the job done. I assume that your sociability must have come from your father, as well. Certainly part of a salesman's success depends on sociability.

Yes. He was very sociable. He loved to talk, to entertain, and especially in business, to convince.

He had many friends. He was a wonderful storyteller, a Gaelic wit, which the Québecois respond to. He was always coming home with new stories, although he was often very quiet at home. Home was a chance to relax.

On hot summer days, Mama would suggest he quit work early, and he'd take us to the beach, either at Marchand's, or at Auger's, on the shores of Lake St. Pierre. Actually, Lake St. Pierre was not really a lake; it was simply a widening of the St. Lawrence River, but since it was fifty by one hundred kilometres with 103 islands, it was like a lake. It was shallow, though, because it was not in the channel of the river. The shores were covered with rushes. You had to walk a long way to get to water as high as a child's waist.

I can still see myself sitting on the steps of number 878 St. Ursule Street watching for the car round the corner and then running into the house with the news. There would be a great rush to get everything into the car to get to the beach as fast as we could. My place was in the middle, my brother on my left and my sister on my right, because I was the youngest. So I was always the last one out of the car, and the last one to reach the lake. Terribly frustrating.

When my father worked for the Poissant Cleaners from Trois-Rivières, he did the shuttle between Shawinigan and Trois-Rivières in a company truck, and he had a uniform with leather leggings and cap. Very manly. I loved this virile look. I was very proud of my father in his uniform. One day I had a terrible toothache, and Papa brought me, lying in the truck, to the dentist in Trois-Rivières. A nice outing for a child. Dramatic.

Which one do you look like?

Probably a bit more like my mother, but with some of my father's presence, if I can use the word. My father carried himself very well. He was a bit chubby, he walked a bit slow, but always very straight. Slouching horrified him. He and my mother both were always telling us, "Straighten up!" There could be absolutely no wrinkles in his white shirts, his pants had to be pressed, his shoes shined. Every Saturday, Gilles and I had to shine our shoes—and I mean shine—and pass inspection. Our Sunday suits also. I learned very early to use a comb.

One of the things, oddly enough, that reminds me of my father is the white shirt that I still see the Japanese wearing. Here, in Japan, it is usually the wife who is responsible for these shirts. For my father, it was me and the Chinese laundry.

Ah, yes. The Chinese laundry. Every town across the country, no matter how tiny, had either one Chinese restaurant or one Chinese laundry.

Trois-Rivières had four or five Chinese families.

So we know, then, that Trois-Rivières was a big town. This would have meant progress from the early decades of the century when Chinese men were allowed into Canada to work on the railways, paying a head tax for the privilege, but they were not allowed to bring their families. There were no Japanese in Trois-Rivières then, I imagine.

No. The Japanese were mostly on the West Coast—at least until they were scattered across the country by the internments in the camps during WWII.

Why do you say you and the Chinese laundry were responsible for your father's white shirts?

I was the delivery boy. As children, we frightened ourselves with the apocryphal story that the Chinese stole white children. Why we imagined they would want us, I have no idea.

Our Chinese laundry was on St. Geneviève Street, right beside St. Patrick's School. The owner was very thin, dark-skinned, with jet-black hair. I never heard him speak. It was a mystery. I imagined scenarios: maybe he was mute, maybe he didn't speak French. I would have imagined a Martian the same way.

So I would go into the laundry on tiptoe, handing over my father's white shirts, careful not to get too close to the counter, and watch while, without a word, he traced a sign, a scribble, with a paintbrush and black ink, "India ink." Then he would tear the paper up the middle and give me half—this was the ingenious receipt necessary to retrieve the shirts. That this scribble could have meaning was another mystery. I would deposit my twenty-five cents for each shirt on the end of the counter and fly off with the parcel. Today, knowing the complexity of calligraphy, I understand that he was educated.

What qualities do you think you have of your mother?

Perhaps I got my artistic side from my mother. My mother was very good with her hands. She knitted and sewed—dresses, shirts, blouses, quilts. She even made clothes for me cut down from my father's or my brother's clothes. There was no one better than her in the kitchen, either. Fabulous *tourtière, fricassée de poisson*, a fish dish of my region which won me a cooking competition—I'll tell you about that later.

I can at least comment here on the fact that you're an excellent cook, and I intend to include your recipe for strawberries with black pepper.

I don't give that one away so easily. It is a well-kept secret. It wasn't one of my mother's recipes, however. She was more traditional. Excellent pies, jams, jellies. I wish I had saved some of her recipes. I have to try to recreate from memory to get the taste.

My mother very much fitted the description of the strong woman in the Bible. She had an inventive spirit, a real way of making ends meet—the jams and the jellies are an indication. No one makes these today. My mother also had a taste for the good life—something I can be accused of. I like fine wines, fine dining, fine pieces of furniture. My mother did, too—her taste in clothing, in the household furniture. When she was older, in her sixties perhaps, she did copper enameling. I would have liked for her to paint, but it was not in her. She understood absolutely nothing about mixing colours. The shapes were fine, but not the colours.

Are you the only artist in your vast extended family?

Yes, although both my parents liked art and music very much. I remember Papa arriving home one day with half a dozen oil paintings he had bought to help a poor artist who preferred drinking over eating. They were all landscapes, yellow moons reflected on calm lakes. Nothing special—I do not know who the artist of these paintings was, but my very first painting as a young teenager was a moon reflected on a lake.

There was no question of art lessons, though. No one even thought of it. But my parents did believe that music was part of an education. My father arrived home one day with an upright piano, a small piano, light oak. My sister Jacqueline was given piano lessons. We often played duets, Jacqueline on the piano and I on the violin, and Papa listening with great delight. My father liked music without knowing much about it. Gilles liked to sing. He was like my Uncle Jean-Marc in this.

Jacqueline

You've remained very close to your sister.

Yes, always. From the time we were small children. We didn't just play together and then grow apart; even as teenagers, we had an affinity. She liked music, too; she used to paint. My friends were

Gilles, Jacqueline and Gaston, 1932.

my sister's friends, and her friends were my friends. My brother's friends were not my friends, even though, actually, we are no further apart in age than Jacqueline and I are. He was interested in mechanics, science, chemistry. He became a pharmacist. Also he went to the seminary for high school and his bachelor of arts, a very different path from me. In those days, it was the route to the professions. The students who went to the seminary—boys, obviously—expected to become doctors, lawyers. This is where I met Jean Chrétien, actually. I was there as an outside student, hopping from class to class, to catch up on Latin and Greek so I could enter the Dominican Order. For the others, there was an atmosphere of success.

I met my sister's first husband only twice, the first time when they came to Ottawa to see me just after they were married, and the second time in his coffin. He died of cancer only two and a half years after their marriage. But he had had a sailboat, and she picked up the bug. After he died, she and a friend bought a fishing boat—it was from Gaspé, so it was a sturdy boat—and they fitted it out for sailing. For years and years and years, she sailed. She was a widow, working as a secretary, and very often after work she would call my mother—she was living with my parents at the time—"I'm going out on the boat." She was often out for the summer, and very often, she was by herself. She knew the entire river coast, both sides, from Montreal to Quebec, the depths, the currents, the shallows, the maritime rules, the coves. She has her captain's papers.

Her second husband also loved sailing. They spent many many happy years sailing together.

You've been a great support for her recently.

Yes. Perhaps. You've been to my studio on their property on the St. Lawrence. I stay with them from May to October.

Both of them are retired. We have had wonderful times together. We all love to cook, so each evening, there was good food, good wine, conversation, with the river at our feet. I love to garden, as you know. I landscaped the property, put in bushes, flowers, and the Japanese stone lantern which is the backdrop behind you in the photo I took of you in my garden.

But for the last few summers, the party has been a little dampened, shall we say. My brother-in-law became ill. We'd rush him to the hospital, and we'd bring him back after a few days. He's eighty-three, so I suppose it is not unexpected.

In the meantime, my sister had to have operations on both eyes, so at times I was going to two hospitals. For her, and for him. My sister doesn't drive, and their home is about twenty minutes from any centre for groceries, for the hairdresser, for the post office, for the hospital, the pharmacy…

She sails—understands wind, currents, lanyards, starboard, aft, storms, ports—and she doesn't drive?

She refuses. I tried to teach her once many years ago, and finally she said, "This is the last time. It is too hard on my nerves."

So no art work for you this summer. That must have been at least a little frustrating for someone with such a strong need to create.

Yes, but they are my family. My family is sick. I have to help. That's all.

The Circus and the Eiffel Tower

You grew up pre-war, a very different world from the post-war era I knew, an era of depression, massive unemployment, soup kitchens.

Yes. Exactly my era. I was born right after the 1929 crash, so I grew up before and during WWII. I was seventeen when the war ended. The crash was a fiasco—there were repercussions on the world financial markets for about ten years, and this was when my father was changing jobs. Even though money was very short for everyone, I don't remember that he was ever without work. I don't think that our family ever wanted for essential things, although there was no pocket money and our toys were ones you could make yourself. Toys were rare. Ironically, the new economic take-off was thanks to the war.

Mind you, children are very creative in designing their toys.

Indeed. Play is constructive. It is in this play, which is identification, that a child forms his psyche. I remember playing house with Jacqueline, which meant imitating grown-ups. I would have been three, four, five years old, directed by Jacqueline, the older sister, who was five or six. We carved houses in the snow and called them igloos. We assembled furniture for our house, very primitive, of course: a tiny table, chairs, even a tiny cradle and a solid little rocking chair painted yellow and decorated in red that had been made by my Uncle Onésime. Sometimes I was the father, sometimes I was the doctor.

And cowboys and Indians? This was a prairie war game very popular among five- and six-year-olds—though perhaps not constructive. There were four or five little boys my age, no girls. The majority must have ruled. We played boy games.

I don't remember playing cowboys and Indians, nor do I remember playing war, even though part of my childhood took place during the war. I was not aggressive.

What is your earliest memory?

The earliest? Possibly having my picture taken sitting in a bath. I remember my aunt, Tante Marie, taking the photograph, which everyone else was forced to appreciate too, because she put it in a local newspaper, a happy little boy with pale locks. I was about three years old. Possibly this is where I developed my taste for the *rotenburo*, the outdoor hot spring in Japan.

Another memory is sledding down the hill on cardboard. The cardboard wore out very fast—as did the seat of the pants.

I certainly remember moving to Trois-Rivières into the two-story apartment, I think at 878 St. Ursule Street, in 1936. We were on the second floor, so we looked across a little to the left at the Dominican nuns' imposing red brick convent and down onto their vegetable garden. A great temptation to a six-year-old. A few years ago I confessed to the nuns that I got the roots for my vocation in their garden. For me and my six-year-old friends, climbing over the fence—it was two metres high, so it took some effort—was a daring exploit. Or we would pull a few nails out from the white pickets. Illicit carrots and radishes, fresh from the garden, still cool from the earth, had an enhanced flavour not to be matched by those from our mothers' ice-boxes.

On the other side of the garden, silhouetted as the sun went down, there was the imposing St. Joseph Seminary, a boys' institution. One could attain a bachelor's degree there. The Dominican nuns did the cooking for the students at the seminary, on top of being in charge of looking after the priests. What a load.

The world economy was on an upswing. The cities of Shawinigan and Trois-Rivières, essentially industrial cities, were in full expansion. But it was a very different world. People bought only what they absolutely needed. There were very few stores. I don't remember the ones on 5th Street in Shawinigan, but I do remember the ones in Trois-Rivières very well. There was Zellers, where Jacqueline sold hats part-time when she was a high-school student. Kresges was on Forges Street. The smart Fortin on Notre-Dame Street. We were a long way from the era of shopping centres today.

I remember being addicted to the Eaton's and Sears catalogues when I was growing up in the country. What about you?

Yes, they brought hours of pleasure. There were two, the spring-summer and the fall-winter, and as long as you placed a few orders a year, they sent it. There was everything, almost to the point that it was an education in adult life: tools, dishes, blankets, the latest fashions for adults and, of course, teenagers, a toy section, a sports section…

And what about your artistic endeavours? I know that you started out using your mother's ironing board to draw on, but I presume that after the age of three or four you had moved on.

Yes. Circus management. When I was nine or ten, I decided to organize a circus. The entrance fee was a few nails, new if possible, or clothespins, which could easily be begged, borrowed, or stolen from one of the neighbouring housewives. I don't remember if I allowed them to borrow from my mother. I think that would have been too much like paying me with my own clothespins. The circus was complete; it even had a tiger in captivity. I painted black stripes onto the back of a cat. Live art. It was a stray cat I caught in the back street. Our own cat was not suitable. It was black.

I exhibited my tightrope skills in front of a select crowd, all paying guests, of course. This was a talent which I had developed on the tightrope behind my grandparents' farm, the railroad. I would say that I developed a certain talent for tightrope tricks.

Aside from carving up my mother's ironing board, and creating live art, I constructed the Eiffel Tower and *le Pont de Québec*, the Quebec bridge. This was done with the obvious construction materials, toothpicks, many boxes of toothpicks stuck together with LePage's glue. These were not insignificant constructions. Each piece was about a metre in length or height. You can imagine the cost to my mother in toothpicks. The humidity, though, was the undoing of my creation. As the Greek sage says, everything changes. Nothing is permanent.

Did you have pets at home in the city? I don't mean a cat that would justify itself by catching mice, for instance, or being used for your art projects, but a pet.

Always. We fed, trained, and petted at least four or five dogs, a cat, a rabbit, a little racing cock, and even a dormouse brought back from the country in hiding, courtesy of my cousins from St. Sévère. One of our dogs, Mickey, was extraordinarily gentle and very smart. Sometimes when he was sleeping I would take off running, climbing the stairs very fast and hiding in some armoire or trunk, or under a bed. Then I would call him very softly. When he found me, I don't know who was more impressed, him or me. He had an enthusiastic appreciation of ice cream. During the summer evenings after supper, Mickey would stick close to me, waiting. Finally, I would say, "Shall we go to Ti-Ri?" He would jump with joy. Ti-Ri was the restaurant that sold ice cream. The tradition was that I would buy two, one for him, and one for me, but there was a strict rule that we wouldn't eat his until we got home. All along the road Mickey was not walking, not jumping, but dancing. Once we got home, I would sit on the steps and hold out his cone, which he devoured at lightning speed, and the whole time I was eating mine, he watched me intently, licking his lips. I adored Mickey!

Were you given an allowance? When I was small, the rate was twenty-five cents a week.

In my time, it was two cents a week.

What did two cents do? What did you do with it?

A good deal. Many days before allowance day—it seemed like many days—I would go to the store that sold candies, run by the very corpulent Madame St. Laurent, finally making my choice, which despite my long deliberations was almost always the same: *Lunes de miel*, candies about the size of a dollar coin, a sweet centre covered in chocolate. Two for one cent—a bargain. I don't think they make them any more.

During a trip to Montreal, I also managed to buy a small airplane with my small savings. I bought an aluminium Spitfire in carmine red. It was both wonderful and significant at the same time. But one day—it was Good Friday—tragedy struck. Very symbolic. I was standing on the staircase on the second floor and I accidentally dropped my treasure. A wing broke off. An immense sadness. Again, the lesson: nothing is permanent.

The Old Priest Héroux

Until the Quiet Revolution in Quebec in the 1960s, large families were the rule. It was revenge of the cradle, population growth encouraged by the Church to overcome dominance by the English after 1762. Even so, your parents had only three children, while others at the time may have had seven or eight or fifteen children. You talk of independent thinking on the part of your parents. It seems to me that your parents were ahead of their time in resisting the pressure of the church to produce a child each year.

Religion did not have undue influence in our home. There were no communal prayers, no recitations of the beads, no benedictions before a meal—and all of these were usual with most of my friends' families. The only religious gesture that I ever saw my father make at home was to cut the sign of the cross on the bottom of the loaf of bread with the knife before he sliced it and to get up before sunrise on Easter Sunday to fill a container of Easter water.

I must have been attracted on my own. Every Sunday, we went to eight o'clock mass at the Franciscan church attached to the Seraphic College. It was very close to our house.

In Trois-Rivières, in Japan—it is always the same. The same people sit in the same spots at the same mass. It has always fascinated me. My father had picked a bench near the middle of the church, on the central aisle, on the right side. And that is where we always sat.

During the week, I'd go to church on my own even before school. I don't know why—something about the atmosphere. I was in high school by then.

Gaston, Jacqueline and Gilles, September 1938.

It was a big parish with one priest and three vicars. I knew all the Fathers who celebrated mass, but I had my favourites I went to for confession.

It was very common among the Québécois Catholic families for at least one member to enter a religious order. Was that also the case with your family?

Absolutely. One of my father's sisters, Tante Germaine, is a nun. She went into the society very early in life. She just passed away, at age ninety-six. Two of my cousins became nuns. Tante Marie, the hairdresser aunt who taught me to drive, joined a lay community, something that was new in the fifties. They never wore the traditional long cloaks. She died when she was seventy-eight.

One of my mother's uncles was a priest, *le vieux curé Héroux,* "the old pastor Héroux," as we called him. He had been paralysed by a stroke at a rather early age. We went with our grandparents once a year to visit him in the village of St. Ursule. Not fun for a child. We had to be on our best behaviour. On top of that, Marie Barrette, the housekeeper with the red wig, insisted on hugging me and Gilles. This was before she brought out the carrot cake which was, without fail, rancid and hard. Fortunately, only my grandfather and my father, the men, were treated to dandelion wine which, also without fail, as soon as her back was turned, was emptied into the flowerpots. It was another one of those childhood mysteries. Would more glorious flowers result or would they be transformed into dandelions?

And on the way back home we would have to suffer through with my grandfather's teasing: "So the little boys have kissed the old lady once again."

It was not the old priest Héroux, then, who influenced you in your decision to enter the Dominican order.

No. It was uncle Barthélemy, my mother's brother, a Franciscan, who influenced me the most. Practically my only early memory of him is that he used to like to wrap us in his heavy brown wool cloak. I was about three then. Then he was gone, first to complete his theological studies in Rome, and then to do seventeen years of missionary work in Libya and in Syria. When he came back to Canada in 1947 after the war, I was seventeen.

When I was a Dominican student in Ottawa, Uncle Barthélemy was the Commissioner of the Holy Land and Superior at the Franciscan Convent in Ottawa. I had special permission to visit him once a month. In my uncle, I saw a religious man, "comfortable in his skin," as we say in French, a religious man who had not abandoned or cut off his human side. During these visits, he offered treats of food, cigarettes, books—the visits were a considerable relief from the hardships of a Dominican student. But I also saw a serious monk who enjoyed his religious life. He was a good preacher. I owe him a lot.

You told me about a rather special novena that you and some high school friends did which involved crossing windy, snowy bridges at 5:00 a.m. If there was no undue influence of religion in your home, how did that come about?

Religion was a way of life then, simply part of the day. There were many kinds of devotions: praying with the beads, the thirteen Tuesdays of St-Antoine-de-Padoue, the devotion to Notre-Dame-du-Cap. Everyone had his own. There was creativity. But this feat, I admit, was not a result of my creativity. Two of my friends had decided to do a special, rather elaborate, novena and were so kind as to invite me along.

The plan was to walk all the way to the sanctuary of Cap-de-la-Madeleine, a distance of about five kilometres, for nine consecutive first Fridays of the month. A nine-month plan. Some of those months, obviously, would be winter, and the route was over the bridges on the St. Maurice River. In –20º, –30º Celsius, the cold and the wind was no joke.

And with the windchill factor, the temperature would have been ¯50º Celsius.

Exactly. If we wanted to be back home to have breakfast and get to school, we had to leave around 5:00 a.m. Our parents would still be asleep. In winter, this is the dead of night. The sun didn't rise until seven.

So your religious vocation became clear very early.

Not really. This was simply a youthful, terribly enthusiastic scheme. The irony is that both Gilles and I went to Seraphic College, which was oriented towards a Franciscan religious vocation; Gilles was studying classics, so he was oriented in that direction. In fact, the year that I boarded at Seraphic—I was thirteen, so I was in grade nine—the superiors informed my parents that I did not have a religious vocation. They thought Gilles seemed to. But he was more interested in science, and perhaps the lay life. He turned instead towards pipettes and test tubes.

Batting 50/50

So school was not the highlight of your youth.

My first years were kind of rough. For the first four years, I was at St. François Xavier School at the corner of our street. This was under *les Frères des Écoles Chrétiennes,* Christian Brothers' Elementary. I have very few memories of that experience. I do remember one of the teachers, Monsieur Laperrière. He was thickset, with glasses, and a very heavy shadow even when he was shaved. I also remember drawing period, which was always the high point of the week. Drawing wasn't until two o'clock on Friday afternoon, so you can imagine how long the week was for me. I always got the best grades in drawing, in spite of having to draw with a ruler and a compass.

In grade five, I was sent to another school run by the *Filles de Jésus* nuns, a community of Breton origin. The teaching was superior and the education very distinguished—at least we felt very distinguished. We wore black uniforms with velvet collars and bow ties, brown leather gloves and caps.

I was coming home from school one day when a Monsignor stopped his car—probably a Monsignor, because his red belt was much in evidence: "My son, where do you go to school?" When I told him, he said, "Who teaches there?" Of course, I said, "*Les Filles de Jésus,* the Daughters of Jesus." And he asked, "Did Jesus have daughters?" When I got home I asked my mother if Jesus had daughters. She was flabbergasted that a Monsignor would ask such a question.

The discipline at the school was very strict, but there was something peaceful and safe about it. It was very sunny—large windows brought a lot of sun into the interior, and the floors shone under the sun. The students were the floor polishers, actually: we had to wipe our feet on thick cloth and slide the cloth with our feet to polish the floor. Even then I sensed a difference between my first school and this school where everything seemed clean and in perfect order.

"In perfect order." How like you. Your studio apartment is always in order. So you liked this school, yet you were there only one year.

It may have been financial. My brother had just finished two years of classical studies at Seraphic College, and my parents had to pay to have him boarded there. My sister also went to school. Education was not free in those days—that is, paid through property taxes—as is the case today. Three children in school cost a pretty penny.

I do know, though, that we moved only once, when I was fourteen, but by the time I entered the Dominican Order, I had gone to five different schools. I have never quite understood… all I know is that the teachers would tell my parents: "It would be better if your son went somewhere else next year." It's true, I never liked sitting and listening to the teachers dumping the waste of their courses on us.

Hmmm. A rather telling comment. They may have seen rebellion in your eyes.

But I was not undisciplined. It was more a question of having confidence in myself. I was independent; I wanted to live my life in my own way even then. I was and still am something of an extrovert. But I also had a hearing problem. So I may have appeared inattentive.

Even though your schooling was expensive, your father also paid for violin lessons for you, and piano lessons for your sister.

Education was very important to my parents, and, as I said, in their minds, music seemed to be part of education. I remember very clearly my father saying one day, "I will work and I will pay for whatever course you want to take. It is your inheritance. Once you have your diplomas in your pocket, you will have to fly on your own." Was it not the same in Saskatchewan? Didn't you take piano lessons?

Yes. The ubiquitous piano lessons. My mother taught piano, so I took lessons. We wouldn't have been able to afford lessons, otherwise. But I did not have a "touch." I remember my older sister, who was very musical, with a lovely voice that she never had a chance to develop, being described as having "a touch." Very discouraging. All my siblings were very talented musically. No one ever said, "Linda has a touch."

So far, we're batting 50/50—one school you disliked intensely, and one you enjoyed immensely. What about the next one?

Mixed. Interesting. This was LaSalle Academy with students from all over the city, so there was a harsher discipline, more suited to males certainly. Brother Olivier, the principal, with his bushy eyebrows and his sunken eyes, scared me a little. I was more comfortable with Brother Mathieu's sensitive nature. He taught music; I chose him over Phys Ed. The only way to be exempt from PE was to play in the band, which is how I came to learn to play the clarinet. The others had to march to our band. But again, I was there for only one year. The next year I boarded at the Seraphic College. Truthfully, it was a thankless year. Learning austere Latin declensions, abiding by a very strict timetable, the doors firmly closed, visits from parents allowed only once a month—even though we lived close by. It was the sort of jail I did not enjoy. Balance sheet: fairly negative. I told my parents I was coming home.

Three good points do come to mind, though. In the recreation yard, a steel wire was loosely suspended between two trees. I used it to perfect my balancing act. I also acted in a play, a comedy which I forget the name of. What I remember best about it is that, to the director's great sorrow, one night I jumped one of the lines of text. The third point was Father Rodrigue Larue, who had an ingenious—positively stupefying—method for teaching Indo-European languages.

The Petits, 1762, and the Héroux, 1656

The Québécois are among the oldest European inhabitants of North America, going back to the 1500s, but much of the West was settled only in the 1900s. My mother's parents, for instance, were pioneers in Saskatchewan in 1905. My father came

even later, in 1914, from Russia. How far back do the Petits and the Héroux go?

Funny you should ask. I can give you very precise information—while I was studying in Ottawa, I worked on the family genealogy. On the Petit side, we go back about 250 years. The first Petit, Pierre Petit, established himself in St-Pierre-les-Becquets in 1762, and every subsequent generation of Petits was born in the same village up until the middle of this century. My father was born in St-Pierre-les-Becquets.

Where was Pierre Petit from in France?

He was born at Pellerin, near Nantes, in 1719. He was married the first time in his hometown, but his wife died in 1758, without children, apparently. We know that Pierre arrived in Canada soon after, because we find him in the 1762 census already established in St-Pierre-les-Becquets. The archives mention that he has a house; a wife, Magdeleine Billy, who was born in 1724 and was a widow. He married her on August 17, 1761. There were two sons and two daughters, the widow's children, no doubt; sixty-six acres of land; one horse; and two pigs. So four years after the death of his first wife, my sailor-ancestor had bartered his ship for one wife, four children and some livestock.

Petit is a name you find all over the world. In English, we have the names Small and Little, and in German, we have Klein. I was astonished to see the number of pages devoted to Petit in the telephone book in Paris. I saw a study a few years ago on the most common family names in France—Petit came in third.

Odd. I looked in the telephone book, too, the Montreal telephone book, but I found a dearth of Petits. On the other hand, there are a multitude of Héroux. I know your immediate family is only three children, and at least one family of cousins was twelve children. What about your parents? Did they come from large families?

The Petit lineage is scanty—even in relative terms. From 1762 until the beginning of the twentieth century, each generation produced only one son until my grandparents' generation who, out of their seven children, had four sons. Aunt Gracia is ninety-five and one uncle is eighty-nine. They are still alive. There were daughters in each generation, of course, but daughters don't carry on the family name.

My mother's side, though, is another story. Jean Hérou de Bougainville was born in 1657 in Blonville in Normandy. He married Jeanne Pépin de Tranchemontagne in Trois-Rivières in 1674, exactly forty years after the establishment of the city, the second city in America, following Quebec, in 1604. Jeanne was born in Trois-Rivières in 1656. Their son, Pierre, the first of all the Héroux in Canada, was born in 1675. His family multiplied, shall we say, advantageously. They would be in the thousands by now.

Picasso and Tante Marie

You've said that you had a happy childhood. We see this reflected in your work—we see no blood, no broken bodies, no martyrs or war.

It is evident that the social context has great influence on the sensibility of the artist. As I've said, I have a peaceful character. I do not like violence. My family and social context was of peace and harmony, a normal childhood sheltered from war, revolt, and violence.

So the war was off-stage, in other words.

Yes. We were in school, focusing on adolescent and school activities. I don't really remember hearing talk about the war. The few paintings I did of my childhood reflect that. A peaceful nature plus a social context without war or violence—and there I am. If you look at the work of someone like the German artist Otto Dix, who lived from 1891 to 1969, you have the reverse of what I am. Otto Dix knew war as a soldier and he was left scarred. His works are imbued with violence, with prostitution, with death.

Picasso also reacted strongly to the political events he experienced. His painting, *Guernica*, for instance, was his reaction to the Spanish Civil War in 1937.

Absolutely. In *Guernica*, horror and fear are gigantic forces. In his book of drawings *I Am the Workbook, 110 of 1940,* dated May 31, 1940, when Paris had just fallen to the Nazis, the grotesque, primitive face of Dora Maar symbolizes destruction. One or two months later, skulls appear.

The only real violence I ever saw was related to putting food on the table. I saw how they bled the pigs, collecting the blood to make black pudding, the guts to make sausages, and the bladder to make tobacco pouches; how they killed the bulls—they were stunned first by a hard knock on the head with the back of the axe, and then hung by the sinews of the back legs.

We did not think of this as violence. When Aunt Albertine said, "You young ones go and kill me four or five hens so I can make supper," we made a game out of it. One of us would cut off the head of one of the hens with an axe, but instead of holding on to the hen so the blood could run out, we would let it fly around in the shed, blood flying all over the well-corded wood, until she was exhausted. We found the resulting art work fascinating. Modern art. Pollock *dans la nature.* An installation.

At that time, the majority of the population was rural. Today of course, much of Canada is urban, and there are very few farms like the ones your and my grandparents had—cows, pigs, chickens—

There were pigs on your grandfather's Jewish farm?

No. No pigs on my grandfather's Jewish farm. I was talking about your grandfather's Christian farm. Once some pigs got loose from the Protestant Norwegian neighbour's, though. My grandfather's barnyard of Jewish animals followed the Christian pigs in a string—they'd never seen anything like it.

Farms in those days provided almost everything for basic survival except cloth, needles, coffee, tea, sugar, and salt. In Quebec, if you had sugar maples on your farm, you didn't even have to buy the sugar. Today, though, farms are pretty much one commodity, only grain, only cattle, only chickens—there are farms without even the requisite dog or cat.

Yes. It was marvellous. The simple mention of *une cabane à sucre,* a sugar shack, brings back such memories…the colours, the tastes, the smells—the boiling maple syrup filling the hut, dry wood burning under the large, flat tub containing the boiling maple water, horse dung. When I hear the words "sugar shack," I can taste the fresh maple syrup. I feel the sun becoming warmer; I see the buckets set under the taps in the trees, the buds tinting the bushes and the trees, the fields taking back their colour. Nature coming back to life—and the people coming back to life. It was totally unlike the sharp odours of the city, the hot concrete, the paper factory.

Each summer Aunt Albertine—she was also my godmother—would announce to my mother that I would stay for the week, not to worry, I could wear my cousins' clothes: "You know that one more or less makes no difference." There was no argument from me, of course. The result would be that I'd

Uncle Barthélemy and Gaston Petit, 1953.

spend not one but many weeks with them. There were many in the family, twelve children, bedrooms for the girls and bedrooms for the boys with many double beds. When there were too many of us, an excess of cousins, we slept all together, in a jumble.

We often went fishing or swimming in the "little river" which was mostly dry in summer. Sometimes we'd go to Rivière du Loup. One of the rivers was east, the other west of the farm. At harvest time, we perched on top of the loads of hay pulled by the horses, which were, by the way, my uncle's pride and joy. We had tarts of thick cream covered with maple syrup. We had bread from the outdoor oven across the road. We fed the animals in the barn. The barn was a treasure trove of trunks and armoires, old chairs, tires. A whole world. We made ice cream, hauling the can of cream up from the well, where it was left to keep cool. The well was a big black deep hole that scared me, actually. In the evening, as we got older, we would sit on the porch discussing the mysteries of life.

It was a marvellous childhood. Very rich. A huge family. Some twelve aunts and uncles, all told, and about sixty cousins. The aunts and uncles were very close. My mother and her sister, my Aunt Albertine, were married in a double ceremony in the smart village of Charrette in the county of St. Maurice on a cold day in April, 1926, the 24th, to be precise. Aunt Albertine and her husband went to live on the family farm at St. Sévère once my grandparents retired. My parents settled in Shawinigan.

So your parents were part of the generation that was moving from rural to urban life. In those days, almost everyone had family on the farm. Summer seems to have been reserved for your country life, if I can put it that way.

Not only in the summer. We visited my grandparents on my mother's side in Charette every Sunday, as often as the weather allowed. My father insisted on it, and this was no small effort. We had a car because he was a travelling salesman. We went from early spring, when the roads were so bad that we often got stuck in the mud, until snowfall in early winter, when we were often stuck in the snow, although, fortunately, not always at the same spot. My father would go off to the closest farm to ask for help, and the farmer would hitch up the horses, cursing him: all week the horses work, they deserve at least one day of rest. My father paid the farmer—no comfort to the horses. The next week, we were back. We were well known.

We would arrive at my maternal grandparents' during high mass—we ourselves went to eight o'clock mass in Trois-Rivières so that we could get to Charette just as the clan there was coming out of ten o'clock mass. Immediately after breakfast, we'd get in the car to make the forty-kilometre trip. Mind you, on those old gravel roads, you weren't travelling at sixty miles an hour like you do today. It could take an hour even on a good road.

We were there in time to take out the key from under the mat to open the door. In good weather, we sat on the verandah facing the church across the street. We'd wait and watch as the parishioners came out, nodding in our direction, *Voilà, les Petits sont arrivés!* "The Petits are here!"

I could hardly wait to get back to the garden, so full of living mysteries. Each weekend, I did a tour, pulling off plums, and red and green gooseberries. I was just checking to see if they were sweet yet, you understand.

Quebec farms were laid out very differently from the farms in the West, which were generally on the square, the homestead in the centre in isolated splendour, and at least one kilometre from the closet neighbour. Loneliness was a serious problem. But the Quebec farms were actually organized into villages.

Yes, in Quebec, each farm was a long strip, usually bordered by a river, the original transportation systems, later by the railroad, or a road, so the farmsteads were very close to each other, and would form a village with shops, a church, and so on, all on the road. Gardens, barns, etc., were in a long strip stretching behind the house. The house faced the road. In my grandparents' case, there was a garden behind the house which ended at the railroad track. Two or three trains passed every day. I used to count the cars. Sometimes there were close to a hundred.

So your visits were only to your mother's parents?

After the meal, we often went to my grandparents' old farm—by old, I mean the original Héroux farm—twelve kilometres down the road in St. Sévère. I learned to drive on that particular road, packed earth alternating with gravel. I knew the road by heart. My mother's sister, Tante Marie, an independent woman and a hairdresser by trade—she never married—had bought a magnificent Chevrolet coupe. One Sunday after the meal—this was in 1944—Tante Marie said, "The rest of you can go ahead. Gaston will come with me. He is going to drive." My father was livid. "You're not serious!" But Tante Marie responded, quite calmly, "He is fourteen years old, he is a man, and he has to learn one day. It might as well be today." So I got behind the wheel, played with the three pedals and the gear shift, and we were off.

It was a wonderful scene, worthy of a film. Everyone was waiting at the farm, the grandparents, the aunts and uncles, the cousins, more than twenty in all, gathered on the verandah, watching for the cloud of dust from which would emerge my aunt's black two-seater. We got a hero's welcome from everyone...except my father, who didn't say a word. Five or six years later, though, he sent me on my own to get my driver's license. The official got into the car beside me and asked me to drive around the block, and I got my driver's license. That was how you learned to drive in those days. After that I drove very rarely, only enough not to forget. Father let no one drive his car: his wife and his car, he used to say, were two things he did not lend.

I presume that your parents kept up the contact with their sisters and brothers long after the children left. But at what age did you stop being part of the family visits?

Until I joined the Dominican Order in the summer of 1952. In fact, it is possible that if we hadn't visited the farm and the cousins, I might never have taken up smoking. This makes my father responsible, in a way, for my smoking, even though he tried to stop it.

Don't tell me that you literally learned to smoke out behind the barn.

I am afraid so. You didn't?

No. I smoked in my father's general store. Only once. I was seven.

You stole cigarettes from your father's store?

No. He let us choose. We had an aunt who smoked, and my sisters and I thought she looked so cool. So we went to our mother—woke her up from a nap, actually—and informed her that she should smoke so she would be sophisticated like our aunt. She said, "Why don't you smoke?" So we trotted downstairs: "Mom says we should smoke."I picked out Export A because of the green package, and my older sister picked out Players in the blue package. I don't remember my younger sister's choice.

The Violin, the Clarinet, and the Bad Spill

You said at one point that, looking back, you realized that your parents were quite open-minded for the time.

There certainly was a marked openness to what I would call "culture." I started playing the violin in school when I was ten, but after that, for about six years, I had private lessons from Mr. Gélinas, a bachelor who lived upstairs in a dark, dusty apartment on St. Antoine Street. The section of the apartment was partitioned off by heavy drapes, and I always wondered what he was hiding—I resisted looking, though. To this day, I still wonder.

He must have been quite good as a teacher because I played with the orchestra for a short time. This was at the start of the symphony orchestra in Trois-Rivières. There was one concert a year. I rmember the long practice sessions of Beethoven's Fifth Symphony. I played this particular—long—piece so much that I could play it from memory.

I stopped playing, but I regret it. I'm not sure whether it was a lack of interest, or because of a mastoid operation on my left ear which damaged my hearing. I still have the violin, and I still dream of taking up playing again some day, although probably not with this violin. It had belonged to one of my cousins, Pierre Héroux, who died very young. The violin expired finally after years of the humidity in Japan and, I admit, my lack of care. The label inside says Stradivarius, but violins are like wines. You can't believe the label. Mine was nothing but a copy.

The violin, the clarinet, painting—so you were not keen on physical activity? No hockey? How did you escape that? Don't all Canadian boys, particularly in Quebec, want to be famous hockey players?

When I was older, I played hockey. I was a goalie. I loved it, even though the skates always hurt. They were too narrow. And of course, along with the rest of Canada, I listened to the hockey games on the radio every Saturday night. This was at the time of Les Canadiens, with the invincible Toe Blake and Maurice Richard.

Mind you, to be honest, I preferred skiing. I think I could say that I had a minor career in jumping. Trois-Rivières was particularly renowned for exceptional jumpers, and I decided to give it a try. I can remember the instructor, Coco Levasseur, being there, reminding me to throw myself forward at the moment of taking flight so I wouldn't fall on my back…finally, one had to decide…or not.

Each time I did it, it was magic, but my career had a dramatic end. It was the end of the afternoon. It was snowing lightly. I had already done quite a few jumps. My eyes were tired—a whole day on the slopes: no one wore glasses for snow glare in those days—and it was the grey half-light of dusk. I misjudged the end of the spring-board. I was a fraction of a second too late in the jump; I touched the ground on top of the jump, rebounded, lost my balance—a complete somersault. I did a spectacular tumble down the slope. The result was miraculously nothing but a sprained left ankle. I limped home with my skis on my shoulders. To my parents, I simply said, "Bad spill." They didn't know that I was jumping.

I decided to quit while I was ahead. I didn't think I would be so lucky a second time.

I misjudged you. I apologize. What about summer sports? Were you equally talented—and lucky?

Basketball, tennis, swimming. We played basketball in the industrial building in the exhibition park on the hills; today it is Maurice Duplessis Park. I was captain of the St. Pat's team for a few years. Basketball is a game I really love. It has everything: it's a team sport, it builds endurance, ability, agility…

Swimming and tennis were combined in a way. We played mostly at night, till about midnight, at Pius XIII Park, today John XXIII Park; I played with racquets strung with gut that always broke, although, even so, I have to admit that I was considered gifted. Before we headed home, we would jump in the pool. Sports facilities always seemed to be far from home in those days. There were none of the amenities expected, even demanded, today: showers, cafeterias, uniforms. No question of a shower after our game, or a snack. Or personal transportation. In summer, we went on bicycle, and in winter we went on foot.

Basketball playing ended with high school. Tennis I played until ten or fifteen years ago when I developed tennis elbow, severe bursitis in my right arm. Since the use of my right arm is more important to me than tennis…the end. Not a spectacular end, simply an end.

Gaston, 1948.

English—Yes and No

You went from a city that was ninety-eight per cent French-speaking to Japan. Yet you are fluent in English. When did you learn English?

In high school. My sister Jacqueline had studied at an English school, St. Patrick High School. She was very happy with it, so I was registered at St. Pat's, too.

That was unusual then, surely.

Again, open-mindedness. Parents seldom sent their children to English schools in the 1950s. Mind you, with my career in changing schools, I don't know whether it was because there were no other choices left for me in the city, or whether my parents had a premonition that an apprenticeship in the Shakespearean tongue would open new doors in my life.

When I started school, I hardly knew the difference between yes and no. This even though an English Irish family had lived in the first floor apartment on St. Ursule Street. The husband was employed in the paper factory and spoke a little French, but his wife, not a word. Of the three children, the oldest one, from the wife's first marriage, spoke French fairly well but with a heavy accent. The second was a real French Quebecer, no accent. The youngest had a slight accent. A wide range of assimilation within one family, and in such a French centre. In those days, Trois-Rivières, 98.5% French, was said to be more French than Paris.

Wasn't that difficult? Complete immersion at the age of thirteen?

I don't remember it as difficult. The new French students at St. Pat's had one year of complete immersion in English, which was very intense, and very progressive. The four years of high school on an equal footing with the English students followed. Compared with my other schools, it was a sort of liberation, boys and girls in the same classes—it created more normal relations. This was unknown in the French schools.

The school was run by the Sisters of Assumption; they were all American, and very open-minded. There was a very sane atmosphere, very positive, even to the point that if we had personal questions that we were embarrassed about asking out loud—about sex, for instance—we would ask in writing, no hesitation. The answers came back in writing or were integrated into our courses. Those who had ears could understand. Sister St. Clair in particular, one of my teachers the last two years, helped me greatly in that aspect. But what I retain, their gift, is that life has something very positive, that life is worth living fully. I don't remember being particularly troubled by adolescent problems. The problems of sexual awakening, of orientation, fitted in here and there and started making sense in my life.

You were lucky. I had a PE teacher who was sixty-three years old—she had been a student herself at the school when it opened fifty years before—who had the responsibility of sex education. I remember a lecture—only to the girls—when she said something vague about not letting boys get too close. There was no such thing as sex education as it exists in school today, and parents didn't talk about sex then.

Mine, either. When I reached puberty, I asked my parents about sex after supper one evening. I got the usual response: "Go ask the priest or Dr. Bellefeuille." I chose the family doctor.

Did you date?

We didn't "date," although, I admit, I did have success with the girls. I thought myself very heterosexual, a bit of a dandy, I'm afraid. I had what we called a "sporty look." I expect we were rather innocent. We often had house parties at one of our homes on a Saturday night, usually at my house, I think because my parents enjoyed having us around. There was dancing, jazz or big band, either to the record player, or one of us on the piano. There would be a small buffet, egg-salad sandwiches, cookies, cakes, and soft drinks. Soft drinks were a treat in those days. By 11:00, we were on our way out the door. There was no question of overstepping the mark.

Or, we babysat. Believe it or not, I organized a group of us, girls as well as boys, depending on our class schedules. We charged twenty-five cents an hour. After 11:00 p.m. the price went up to thirty-five cents, and we had to be driven home. The teachers knew everything we were up to. They were always interested, full of questions for us on Monday morning—"How was the party?" "How was babysitting?" Well, everyone knew what we were up to.

The fact of living like an "old bachelor" changes many things. I like meeting people and I have many friends of both sexes, of different ages, different cultures, you name it—probably an attitude passed on by my parents. My choice having been made, though, there has never been a question of living with anyone. My studio is my private space.

So high school, at least, was a successful period. I presume that you were a good student.

Very good, thank you. Right from the start of the second year of high school, I opted for classical studies. I was at the top of my class, but there was very little competition. Out of about thirty students enrolled at the start, the ranks thinned out very fast. Just seven students received their diplomas in 1950, and only two, Romeo Paré, another Frenchman, and me, were boys.

The Lost Scout Troop and Harry Potter's Nimbus 2000

You are famous, I understand, for both losing and saving the same cub troop. First, how did you come to be part of a cub troop at all? I remember you saying that you weren't a joiner. No organized kid stuff.

I didn't really join the Scouts. I was enlisted, and I was nearly twenty, about to finish high school. The St. Pat's troop needed a leader; I was asked, and for some reason it didn't occur to me to say no. I had some very basic Scout training, and, voilà, I was the leader of a delightful troop of twenty young folk. There was the prerequisite camping, and even a jamboree at Vaudreuil. It rained, it rained cats and dogs, all during the jamboree. When my parents came to visit, my father had tears in his eyes: "Why are you going through such misery?"

Of course, the rain wasn't my fault, but I am forced to concede that I was responsible for the next adventure. Or misadventure. I took twelve of my Scouts on a cross-country ski trip, along with—who was it now? It might have been my friend Max. I was constantly enlisting him for my adventures. My famous 1000-kilometre bike trip, for instance.

So, it was the 30th of December, a good way to end the year, I thought, and it was a thirty-three-kilometre trail. The trail began at the last village on the edge of the wilderness. The trail followed a series of little lakes through the forest at the foot of a mountain, and then over the mountain. I had checked that this trail actually existed, and I had alerted the village of St. Jean des Piles on the other side of the mountain at the end of the trail. We were expected. But no matter how clear the trail was on the map, it was impossible to find, and then night fell. We heard the church bell in the distance, finally, which oriented us like the proverbial Boy Scout compass, but it was too late. It would be too difficult to return in the dark, and too dangerous. I decided we would stay put—without shelter, without food. Anything we had had to snack on was long gone. I kept the boys busy cutting down pine branches to make a bed around a fire which we kept going all night, and we slept with our feet to the fire. We filled a tin box with snow and set it to melt by the fire, and I gave the order that anyone who woke up was to warm up by drinking some of the warm water. My assistant—Max?—and I took turns keeping watch.

At first light, we woke everyone up with a sharp Boy Scout whistle, and retraced our steps to the village. At the first house we came to, there was a farmer harnessing his horse who felt sorry for us and took us to the bus stop on his sled. Surprisingly, no one became ill. And you should have heard these young heroes once we got back to the town.

Gaston Petit, "le beau garçon," 1951.

They had heard owls in the night, seen wolves... Thus are legends born.

Let's go back to this 1000-kilometre bike trip you refer to.

This I blame on my new bicycle, an earlier version of Harry Potter's Nimbus 2000. When I was about fifteen, my father insisted that my brother Gilles and I work during summer vacation to earn our own spending money. The result, in the spring of 1947, was my first bicycle, a spanking new light green three-speed CCM. It was so beautiful—what could one do but fly away on it? I enlisted my friend, Max Levesque. I wanted to ride to Ottawa and back, and my plan was that we would go into training. So every Saturday afternoon, we rode from Trois-Rivières to Shawinigan on the old road with its magnificent hills and marvellous views. The roads were narrow and winding: our parents did not endorse this scheme with our same enthusiasm. The goal was Tante Marie's house at the height of Côte St. Marc, where we were rewarded with a very healthy glass of milk.

We pedalled off to Ottawa on a beautiful summer morning, a small tent in my basket and an odometer attached to the wheel of the bicycle. During the entire six days of the trip, I don't remember any rain at all—bad for the farmers, perhaps, but good for us. One night we slept in the tent near a farmer's house. People were very kind. In Ottawa, we stayed with my Franciscan Uncle Barthélemy, who was delighted to see us, if a little surprised. We also called on one of our former babysitting clients, Deputy Minister Léon Blacer. He gave us tickets to sit in on a session of parliament: the experience wasn't exciting enough to attract either of us to politics.

We didn't want to come back on the same route, so we consulted the map—Ottawa was only eighty-five kilometres from Prescott and the American border on the other side of the St. Lawrence. We could go through Ogdensburg, New York. and back through Cornwall, Ontario. We had another beautiful day. We were a little nervous at the border, but we were only asked a few questions, our papers were glanced at, and we were through. Nothing strange about boys on bicycles, apparently. We were very extravagant and slept at a bed and breakfast in a small village in New York State one night. There was a sign in front of a house; the owner was sitting on the verandah. We shouted from our bicycles, "How much?" For only five dollars each, one of the best meals, showers, and sleeps of my life. But the next day, we were back on the road. I remember being very respectful of the Cornwall canal, which seemed too close for comfort.

Then there was the stress of following Sherbrooke Street to cross Montreal one Saturday towards noon—this after all the idyllic country roads, woods, streams, birds. By the time we got to Berthier that afternoon, we had done the daily 130 kilometres we had set for ourselves, but Trois-Rivières was scarcely sixty-five kilometres away, so we kept on going. When we got home that evening, we had done 220 kilometres in one day. 880 kilometres from Monday to Saturday. Now, even to me, it feels legendary.

Un beau garçon plutôt mondain: Party Animal

There is a description of you as a youth in an article by Guy Robert as "un beau garçon plutôt mondain," basically, if you don't mind me putting it this way, a gorgeous guy who was also a bit of a party animal. You surprised everyone by entering a religious order.

It is not such a mystery, I think. I was idealistic. I was searching, and I was excited by everything. It wasn't only art. I also played the piano, the violin, and the clarinet. I read a lot. I was deeply impressed by Antoine de Saint-Exupéry, by the symbolism and poetry of his *Le petit prince,* and *Vol de nuit*, where de Saint-Exupéry tries to find meaning in action, moral values in modern society. There was also the humanism of Albert Schweitzer's *Out of My Mind and Life.* For me, Schweitzer encompassed all: he was a theologian who wrote on St. Paul. He was an artist—his specialty was Bach on the organ. He was a man of action. He had spent his life as a medical doctor and missionary in Africa. Someone else who had a profound effect on me was Thomas Merton, with his book, *The Seven Story Mountain.* Merton bridged the artist, the monk and the mystic. I could say that Merton led me to see that such an idealistic life was possible. I was in my teens then, maybe seventeen, eighteen.

Then out of the blue—one might call it Providence—I came upon something else, a booklet explaining the Dominican Order. It seemed to summarize what I had been looking for: a solid education in scripture and theology, preaching in all its forms, and a sense of liberty. But I had to keep on studying. I didn't have the qualifications. At that time, you needed a BA degree, so in order to be admitted as a novice, I had to do a further two years of study of Latin and Greek, which I did at the Seminary of Trois-Rivières. I finally entered the Dominican Order in 1952 at twenty-two, although my education was very different from a novice whose BA had been focused from the beginning on a religious career. I graduated in 1956, at twenty-six, in philosophy. Three years later, at the age of twenty-nine, I was ordained as a priest. I graduated in theology the next year, in 1960, after eight years of very strict training.

By "strict," I assume that you mean "disciplined."

Yes, highly disciplined. I came to the realization through that experience that freedom is recognition of your boundaries—expandable boundaries. I'm sure you've come across people who were physically confined, yet their inner self, the spirit, was free—people like the brilliant British physicist Stephen Hawking, or Helen Keller, or some long-term prisoners. Nelson Mandela, perhaps. Joining meant agreeing to follow a set of rules, harmonious and time-tested. Our only free time to do as we pleased was on Thursday afternoons. Yet I never felt that I was in a prison of any kind. We had prayer, study, meditation, exploration of the inner life. In brief, discovery of another world, that of the spirit, that of the mind, that of trying to tune in to the Absolute, whatever Its name may be: the Nameless for some, God for others... It was totally absorbing, absolutely entrancing. I knew that once that period was over, my physical freedom of

Gaston Petit as a Dominican novitiate, 1952.

Gaston Petit at study, 1954.

movement would expand outward naturally. I was free to join the Order. I was free to leave if I could not or did not want to adapt to such an orderly life.

Today the education for the Dominican Order has changed drastically. The regime of silence, for instance, has gone. I don't say for better or for worse. Simply that the training is different.

Can you describe what those years were like?

Silence was a rule.

Total silence?

No. You're thinking of the Trappists. Their lives unfold in total silence.

So what was a day in the life of a novice or of a Dominican student?

We arose at 5:30 for breviary chants, meditation and mass followed by breakfast. Classes were from 9:00 to 12:00, followed by the chanting of psalms. Then the noon meal, and then recreation, an hour of volleyball, tennis or hockey—the first time our silence could be broken. We had personal study until 5:00 p.m., then vespers, meditation and the evening meal, no speaking during meals. There was twenty more minutes of recreation, during which we were allowed to talk. There were evening prayers. Lights were out at 9:30. It was mandatory.

During the noon and evening meals, there were always readings. At lunch, there was a reading of some subject of general interest. I remember a book called *Ibn-Saud* about the life of the king who created Saudi Arabia. During the evening meal, there was another reading, but from the lives of the saints, spirituality. After the first year of learning the way of the Dominicans, prayers, and so forth, there were three years in philosophy, psychology, metaphysics, logic, and the history of philosophy—pre-Socrates to Aristotle, the mediaeval philosophers and the moderns, Heidegger,

Spinoza, Bergson, Sartres, Lavel. The ultimate purpose was to develop a personal thinking, to form our own opinions and defend them. The professors at the Dominican House of Studies in Ottawa wanted us to react personally to what they were teaching us.

What was the purpose of the silence?

To come to know oneself and to think for oneself. If we were to have something worthwhile to give, we first had to learn. The goal, in short, was to follow the path of St. Dominic, to balance contemplation with action.

Do you really think people will be interested in such mundane detail?

I would hardly call the description you have just given of eight years of a life of silence, meditation, and study as mundane. Were these eight years of training with the Dominicans at all difficult for you?

They were. Especially at first, having to wear a heavy old wool garment which had previously been worn by some other *religieux*, along with yellowed socks, and rough wool shirts. The food was a problem at first—it was almost totally vegetarian—although I adapted quickly enough. The continual silence, though—there were many disputes among us we had to try to sort out. To do that in silence...

Because it was a life organized entirely around a scholastic and liturgical schedule, time seemed to take on another dimension. We were completely removed from the outside world, living in the world of the self. No newspapers, no radio—and certainly no television.

Okii

I presume that during your eight years of study, art disappeared from your life completely.

Not completely. On our Thursday afternoons off, one of the things I did was check out whatever exhibitions were on. This was new. In my little city of Trois-Rivières, there was no such thing as art classes, art teachers, art galleries, or art museums. Our family went to Montreal only once a year to visit relatives, so there was no possibility of visiting an art museum there, either.

I remember a very large painting in tones of cream and brown at the National Gallery. It was by Sugai, a Japanese artist living in Paris. I stood hypnotized in front of that canvas. It drew me, enveloped all of my being. I can still see it: a form which came from the kanji character *okii*, "immense" in Japanese. Was it a sign? I don't know. At that time, I was very far from any thought of ever living in Japan.

Sometimes on those Thursday afternoons, I would meet with a friend, Paul Moore, who was studying at the Capucin House of Study fifteen minutes' walk from us. This was the Franciscan Order. Our two orders sometimes used to play hockey on those Thursday afternoons. Paul taught me the basics of silkscreen printing, inks, how to use the squeegee to spread the ink. But this was far from what one considers as signed and numbered editions. At the time, there was no such thing.

What happened to him? Did he continue in art?

Paul does social work now, counselling young people who want to get off drugs. I think he long ago left art behind.

So despite having had no formal training in art, you leaped directly into professional work once you arrived in Japan.

You're right. I never had any formal training in art, except for the two years in calligraphy under Hidai Nankoku, and my brief studies in *sumi-e*, which ended very abruptly over a leaf of bamboo.

You're right. What I know about art I learned on my own.

My "pleasure" is first the challenge of discovering how something is done, and then testing out this knowledge and putting it into application. Etymologically "art" comes from the Latin *ars*. "Art" has the meaning of *manière de disposer, de combiner habilement*, to combine elements with clear judgment, wisdom, and ingenuity. For me, the challenge of the discovery of the "how to" is part of creativity, fosters creativity. It is probably because of this that I was able to teach. Before I could do it, I had to first analyze it clearly. This was the case for painting, printmaking, stained glass windows, murals....

Sometimes it feels almost like a sixth sense. I look in books and magazines a lot, and when I come across art pieces I try to figure out how they were done. I observe, I sniff around, and—I go ahead. Before I did the paper wall in Kyoto in 1963, I had never done any kind of mural or interior design. The two murals, one ceramic and the other in concrete, at St. Albert Convent in Montreal were also a first. I had never done anything in stained glass, small or large, before the stained glass windows in the church here in Shibuya, and these windows in the church cover more than 1000 square metres. I made sketches first in colour pencils, then in transparent polyester. When I was happy with the drawing, I sent it to a company in Germany to have them done. I had never done a metal mural when I was asked by St. Mary's International

Arthur, Antoinette and Gaston, 1953.

Gaston and Jacqueline, 1958.

School. I contacted somebody who worked in metal and asked him how to proceed. He suggested that I make the forms in styrofoam. And they were cast.

My second exhibition in Paris was of prints. I remember a man standing for a very long time in front of a print called *Des rêves auxquels je reste rivé.* I went up to him: "This print seems to please you." He responded with a question: "How was it made?" "It is a lithograph." "That is impossible." "No, I made it myself." He refused to believe me: "It is not possible. I work at Mourlot, and our workshop could not make this print." I simply answered: "Thank you."

For me this was the highest compliment. Mourlot is where all the big names in art in the fifties and sixties were printed, Chagall, Picasso—this was the most renowned print workshop in the world.

II

THE APPLE, THE BIRD, AND THE PARASOL: THE COLLECTIVE UNCONSCIOUS

Art, as Gaston Petit says, is a big word: in his search for definition he travelled for two years throughout Asia and Europe, visiting with Krishnamurti in Madras and exploring existentialism in Paris. His search took him to Jung, to Buddhism and Hinduism, to death—and it all began with his mother's ironing board.

Comic Books and Ironing Boards

What is your first memory of art?

Art is a big word. If you ask me, "How did you start doing something which is related to drawing, to art in a very general way?" I would answer that my first attempts at drawing go back to when I was three or four years old. I remember drawing on my mother's wooden ironing board with a pencil. In fact, I went so far as to carve these *petits bonhommes*, "little people," in the wood. A vertical rectangle for the body topped by a circle as the head. I won't comment on the symbolism attached to the rectangle and the circle.

I think my mother was afraid of an invasion. First she tried to restrict me to one section of the ironing board—"Don't spread them all over!" Then she supplied me with paper and coloured pencils—they were the only art supplies available at the time, anyway—and I started drawing cartoons, simple, geometrical black lines filled in with solid colour. I was crazy about cartoons. They were in the weekly colour supplement of the Montreal newspaper, *La Patrie*. My first studies in art. I drew on the back of my father's business correspondence: Blondie and Dagwood, Mickey Mouse, Maggie and Jigs, The Katzenjammer Kids; in French, Toto et Titi.

I'm not gifted as a cartoonist, but I see the influence of comics in my art. I realized only recently that my stained glass windows and many of my paintings which are essentially line drawings filled with flat colours are using the same basic cartoonist techniques of my youth. My very early youth. Am I closing the circle?

You say that "art" is a big word. How do you feel about the word "artist"?

All definitions are restrictive. Let's look back at what people, certain people, have done. In prehistoric cave paintings in France, we see the work of people who even then were *transcribing* what they were seeing. By doing that, they were *transforming* what they saw. They saw more than the senses perceived. From a lump of clay or a stone—in other words, some element from their environment—an idol, a sculpture, was fashioned. With charcoal or diluted coloured clay, a line was drawn which became a bison. The same creative gesture was repeated over and over, developing the skill to appeal to the imagination. Obviously "the skill to appeal to imagination" is crucial in art. Picasso *transformed* bits of string, paper and metal with a skill that appeals to the imagination, giving us the essence of the guitar. I might affix a CD behind the head of an Inuit sculpture which then becomes St. Dominic.

The artist is a receptacle of emotions coming from no matter where: from the earth, from the sky, from the sea, from two pieces of fruit, from anything. An artist works by necessity, much like a child constructing his castles in the sand. The child does not play, he invents his universe. The painter also invents his universe. He paints as if he has an urgent need to discharge himself of his sensations and his vision.

The artist's role, then, is to repeat the creative gesture in such a way as *de faire vivre l'essence des choses*, to bring to life the essence. He is a magician, a sort of demiurge who *transforms*, *metamorphoses*, in a way which answers to his sensibility, to his spirit, to all of his being, no matter whether he draws with a simple crayon or pencil, with pigment, with a piece of earth or with a stone. To give another meaning, a new meaning, to elements with the skill to appeal to the imagination,

Stained glass window, Shiroyama Church, Nagasaki, 2000.

is the characteristic of an artist. This is artistic creativity.

When I was out on errands in Shibuya a few years ago, I was struck by piles of discarded packing styrofoam thrown on the sidewalk in front of electronic stores. They meant something special, they sparked artistic possibility. Cut and reworked, the styrofoam became sculptures worthy of being cast in metal. Another time I bought three styrofoam eggs the size of ostrich eggs. I painted designs on them in oils. These paintings became part of the series *Mémoire d'homme*. Does one think of these first as eggs, or as paintings?

Old Bags, Paper Bags, and Kimonos

So your inspiration for your art really does come, as you say, "from no matter where."

Let's disregard the word "inspiration" for now. An artist has a sensibility. He reacts to something—a situation, an object, an idea that might appear to be very trivial to others. There is no specific point of reference. It usually starts with a kind of "click" in the subconscious. Once the spirit is "awake," one has the impression that it is receptive, waiting. Receptive to what? I don't know. The spirit of the artist is awake, waiting in a state of readiness, what I would call a state of grace, to receive something inexplicable that one calls "inspiration." That is the preparation.

One day I had two oranges which I had left on my table, and there was a spark. The colour, the shape, even the smell of the oranges meant something particular. I took a small canvas and painted them. Another canvas followed, then another and another, a total of twenty-two canvases painted in only a few days, till the two oranges rotted. I simply could not extend the series with other oranges. The *Oranges* series had come to an end. Years later I did something similar in my studio in Champlain with three bell peppers, one yellow, one red and one green.

Another time the meaning of two Japanese characters sparked a reaction. There is an expression in Japanese, *O-Fukuro*, "Mummy," "Mom," or "my mother," which has a very warm connotation. This is an expression that a man, not a woman, can say in reference to his own mother. But together the two kanji characters compose an expression which reads "noble bag." I was shocked. My Latin background, maybe my family background, too, would not allow me to accept such—I don't know, disrespect—even though I know that in English there is the expression "old bag," and not necessarily with warm connotations, either.

So the expression *O-Fukuro* was a shock which provoked an artistic reaction. I first made a small painting depicting an object, half bag, half female torso. Another larger painting followed, then another, then the shopping bags became the object of paintings, and finally there were shopping bag collages. I *transformed*, *metamorphosed*, the shopping bags from mere containers used for carrying, to objects that appeal to the imagination. To works of art.

Let's take the kimono, then, as an example of giving new meaning.

Good example. *Étendards un jour, étendards toujours* is a work which is highly symbolic, even as to the placement of the work in a gallery. There are three kimonos mounted on wooden forms which form a triptych. These are actual kimonos that I pulled apart, glued onto wooden panels, and painted over. One was a wedding kimono for women, which is why it is so large. An "everyday" kimono for men. And one of my own cotton yukatas. The centre panel is a white kimono with a shape like a red arrow pointing upwards, touching a black space. On the back, a large sun emerges from a black maze. This large panel is flanked by two smaller ones, one mostly gold, the other mostly black—a crucifixion. White, symbol of Christ. Wound in black. Red, the blood. The red arrow is the blood that flows from the black wound, while on the back, the sun of resurrection emerges from the shadows of evil.

During exhibitions, the triptych is placed facing the entrance of the gallery. In terms of symbolism, this is a strategic location. The work now serves as did screens of yore, the *tatebyobu,* which were placed at the entryway of houses in Japan and China to repel bad spirits. It was believed that bad spirits can travel only in a straight line, so when they hit the screen, they are hurled back.

Bad spirits aren't very bright.

No. People, though, go around the *tatebyobu*. People are more intelligent. Or perhaps we can equate them with the good spirits, who are not stopped by the *tatebyobu.*

So I have given the kimono, thought of as merely a garment, a new use. A new meaning. We are forced to see these kimonos out of context. In a new way.

Are you always conscious of where your inspiration comes from?

No. Probably like most artists. With most of my work, I'm not sure of the precise "click." Or perhaps it is simply that I do not think about it. I am not inclined to delve too deeply in the meanderings of the subconscious when I speak of my art. There is always a "mysterious" aspect in creation which defies definition. While a work is being made, it follows the mobility of thought. Finished, it changes further according to the individual who looks at it. A work of art always changes, since it lives only through the individual who looks at it. The Sistine Chapel, for instance, lived differently when Michelangelo painted it than now, even if it has regained its pristine colours, because when we look at it now, it is in a different context.

The sources of inspiration for one painting I am sure of, though, is my sunflowers, *Trade Hits Outside of Frame.* It was neither the colour nor the shape of the radiant sunflowers in Van Gogh's painting that provoked mine. It was the purchase of his *Sunflowers* by a Japanese insurance company at the absolutely aberrant price of seventy million dollars. True, Van Gogh's *Sunflowers* are splendid, but do they justify the price? My reaction, my comment, was a canvas including Van Gogh's sunflowers in front of Hokusai's red Mount Fuji. Van Gogh had signed "Vincent" on the vase containing the sunflowers. On my canvas, on the same vase, in the same spot, I signed Gaston.

Henry Argall and Henri-Paul Pleau, the Postman

You paint in oils, you do prints, sculptures, murals, stained glass windows—what did you start with first? What was your route?

The route? I first started doing scribbles, doodles, then drawings, then paintings. I remain forever indebted to Henri-Paul Pleau, a postman in Trois-Rivières. Monsieur Pleau gave me hints on where to buy materials, how to mount a canvas, how to start a painting. After that, I took my brushes and painted. I used to go to his house on my bicycle with my friend, Henry Argall—a Frenchman, as we say, in spite of his name. Henry was about thirteen or fourteen, the same age as me. His father, who was very old, was of English origin. Henry was already an excellent painter. He knew how to paint a Corot landscape like nobody. Henry was one of the most talented artists I have ever met. He played the piano—classical, popular, jazz, boogie woogie... He taught me very simple chords and how to jazz them. After that, I learned by ear. Henry Argall also gave me my first tubes of oil paint, a little chest containing tubes of oil paint. My first contact with oils.

I remember my very first painting, a landscape, painted on a square of masonite. A moon reflected on the surface of a pond. The reflection was the colour of silver. I didn't have any white paint in a tube, so I used whatever I could find around the house. A leftover commercial paint, silver coloured. We have to put ourselves back into the context of the times: it was the end of the war, only very basic materials were available, and there was no money to buy even those.

I threw my first painting in the fire a few years later. The memory came back to me long after. I was watching the film *Citizen Kane,* the sequence where they are throwing Kane's belongings into the fire after his death—the sleigh, the painting—destruction by fire. They had become souvenirs, objects, and fetish objects—fire consumes the objects. Memory makes them into a phoenix.

There is only one of my early canvases left, a bad painting, dated 1944 on the back, the Bellemare family home, a red house that I used to see when we were driving away from my grandparents' home in Charette. I have bequeathed the painting to the Pierre Boucher Museum in Trois-Rivieres.

What happened to Henry?

He went on to study art in Montreal and then in Europe, but maybe he was too talented. He had a career in neither art nor in music. He became a hairdresser, and he was blind when he died. Talent is not everything. You have to cultivate it, work it with a will in order for it to result in something.

You say that Henri-Paul Pleau the postman got you started. To what extent?

Monsieur Pleau was a very warm person, happy to share his knowledge. He taught me the ABC's, how to make my own brushes, how to prepare the canvases... I made the brushes with my mother's or my sister's hair, a little bit of metal from a can, a stick and some glue to keep everything in place. For the canvases, he directed me to the Wabasso factory on St. Maurice Street to buy cotton canvas, then, once it was stretched on a frame made of wood strips, soak it with a mixture of glue made from fish melted in the saucepan—the nauseous odour permeated the whole house—and white lead. For the paint, Monsieur Pleau told me to buy oil colours in paste that the commercial painters used to mix with the white. The main base colours were sold only in quarter-litre sizes. There was only one art merchant in the city, anyway, and his choice of materials was very limited.

On the technical/artistic side, Monsieur Pleau gave me advice on the construction of a scene, elementary things, for example, when it comes to a landscape or an inside scene, to start with what is furthest, the background—the sky in a landscape, the wall or back scene for a still-life—and not to be scared to use complementary colours. To tell you the truth, this was all given in a few lessons, two or three meetings at the most.

When I was studying in Ottawa for my ordination as a priest, I got the basics in silk screening and inks from a another student, also studying to become ordained as a priest, Paul Moore from the Capucin Order.

But you did not think of yourself as an artist at that time, I gather.

I don't think so. But even though it was not continuous, I loved working. I remember making copies of paintings without worrying about the exact size of the works—Gainsborough's *Blue Boy* and Rigaud's *Louis XIV*, I think, a head of Christ, and a profile of Pope Pius XII, just as he appeared on the cover of a newspaper. Learning how to use the colours, what shade for the long stockings and the royal blue coat bordered in ermine, how to shade the details of the Pope's aquiline nose and of his smile... In truth, I painted as an amateur, and in sporadic fashion.

Yet you did work towards having a show—your first show was just before you came to Japan in 1960.

That was perhaps a matter of circumstance, more than intent. I wanted to have a pastoral experience before I went to Japan to join the Dominican Order here in Shibuya, so I spent the summer, this was the summer of 1960, as a substitute chaplain in the Canadian Air Force. I was first at the Vancouver military base, then at the radar base in Holberg. It was on the tip of Vancouver Island—a real rainforest jungle, constantly wrapped in fog. It didn't take long to figure out that I'd have plenty of spare time, so I brought quite a few canvases along with me. Sundays were exacting, with bilingual services, and fasting from midnight to noon. The men were rather rough. On Monday, though, I might climb onto a plane for an outing in Vancouver for the day. It was an attractive career, but not attractive enough to change my mind about my original project of going to Japan.

Can you imagine me wearing a captain's uniform? Cap, epaulets, and the military salute? Back in Trois-Rivières I had my first show after my assignment as chaplain. Since then, I have had exhibitions, mainly prints—they're cheaper to ship—in many foreign galleries. I have participated in almost all of the large juried international biennial exhibitions since the end of the 1960s: Barcelona, Spain; Yorkshire, England; Cracow, Poland; Biella, Italy; Frerikstad, Norway; Frenchen, Germany; Burnaby, Toronto, Canada; and Ljublana, Yugoslavia.

Gaston, air force chaplain, Station Vancouver, 1960.

Art vs. Religion

What comes first for you, art or religion?

I was born an artist. In a sense I can't say that it is my fault. It's a gift I received. I recognize it as such, and I am grateful for it. I have to confess, though, that during my adolescence, I never thought that I would spend my life as an artist, to preach by art. In Canada, I was painting as a hobby, you understand. There was never any time for anything else. That continued in Japan: right from the beginning, I was simultaneously studying calligraphy, the Japanese language, and Japanese culture. Painting was only in my spare time.

But after I designed the stained glass windows for our church in Shibuya—1000 square metres, so not an inconsiderable project—the Fathers of St. Viateur of Kyoto asked my advice. They were planning the construction of a chapel for the school campus. This was before the Tokyo Olympics, before Vatican II, and before construction of the super-rapid Shinkansen. It took six and a half hours on the train to reach Kyoto from Tokyo, compared to less than three hours today.

I understand that the Viatorians were not enamoured with your suggestion.

They were not. An architect from Osaka, Shingo Maotani, had already drawn up plans in the "little church with belfry" style that we see in the countryside of Quebec. I objected. This absolutely did not suit Kyoto's architecture. Also I saw drastic changes in liturgy coming in the wake of the 1964 Vatican Council, removing the altar from the wall in order to celebrate the mass with the priest facing the congregation, delivering the service in the language of the people rather than in Latin, and so on. The Fathers listened to me with a certain stupefaction, and then they referred me to the Bishop who I believe they expected to support them. Fortunately—he was a great man with an open mind—he gave me full authority. I worked very hard to do something innovative—murals, altar panels, tabernacles. I had a lot of help in the construction of the mural from the students in the boys' school, who were absolutely delightful to work with.

Gaston in Bruges, 1965.

When the chapel was finished, it caused quite a commotion, but it became a post-Vatican II model. The result was that I was approached by my Dominican superior with a very generous offer: "If you want to be a religious artist, you can orient yourself in that direction."

And you jumped at the opportunity.

I am not so much of a jumper. I asked for a period of reflection. I could sense my need in that direction. My studies in calligraphy were opening up a whole new way of looking at art—pushing me from the figurative to the abstract. I was feeling more and more drawn, but I needed time. I asked for permission to travel to Europe. I was gone for two years, 1963-65, and on the route from Japan to France, I visited most of the countries that were open to visitors. I was a little like a pilgrim, gleaning all I could gather in my travels about the influences on Japan, ways of thinking, visual, and other influences. I was truly completing my cultural and artistic education, and I was also testing out my ideas. I was painting as well. I had an exhibition in New Delhi. I lived almost a year at Anthony near Paris in lodgings in a very ancient house with space to work in the loft, very *sympa* as the French say, that gave me a show at Gand, Belgium, and another one in Paris. All this was mixed in with visits to museums, to galleries, to ancient churches and new ones, seeing as many as I could of those being built in the post-council style. And all the time, I was considering my superior's suggestion.

You asked which came first, art or religion. In my travels through India, Cambodia, Thailand, it was clear: art and religion are not separate in these countries. Man needs images, lives with and through images. While making his "religious" art, the artist gives all that he has of himself. The Gupta sculptures of the Buddha, for instance, are so ethereal, so spiritual in their simplicity. During my travels, studying the narrative images on temple walls, on church doors, on scrolls, I questioned myself constantly: couldn't I do the same? Attain a similar degree of spirituality while doing my art? Through my art? Observing how artists of other religions developed in their iconography, and their narrative images, the elements, the material they used, how they express their belief.... Couldn't I work in the same spirit within my own faith?

Religion, the faith I belong to, is indissolubly linked with my art. It is impossible to separate them now.

That's different from seeing yourself as a medium, a voice of God.

Definitely. I am not the charismatic type, the prophetic type. I search for the truth in order to be able to transmit it. Of course, you can now be like Pilate asking Jesus: "What is truth?" I am still searching. I don't have an answer.

Art: Nostalgia for God

When you design for a church—a mural, stained glass windows, a tabernacle—you are thinking of a religious site. In that sense, the work is religious. Do you consider your other work, paintings and prints, for instance, as religious?

You are not the first to ask this question. In 1981, my superior was visiting in my studio. I was working on *L'oreille au guet, The Listening Ear.* He watched me work, and finally he asked—with some amusement, actually: "When are you going to do religious paintings?" I could have answered, I suppose, in philosophical terms. This—he is a trained philosophical scholar, after all—he would have understood quite easily. Alex von Jawlesky, for example, defines art as nostalgia for God.

Art is nostalgia for God?

The search, the creation, is a way to go back to God, the Alpha, to reach God, the Omega. As both an artist and as a man, I have a nostalgia for home, a craving. God can never be defined or narrowed down to any fixed notion or point: this nostalgia becomes the push, the motor, which compels the artist—the artist in me—to work, to work, and work again, never able to achieve the defining image which contains all the others. Only God contains all. An impossible search, after all. It is not possible to appreciate and understand all of God's riches, or to understand the Mystery or the Finality. No religion can. Each religion depends on the culture out of which it was born.

But you didn't say this to him.

No. I went directly to the point: the painting we were standing in front of. "Observe well," I said, "the elements of this canvas." Then I sent him home: I sat down and a few hours later, I handed him a treatise. In the first place, in full centre, we see a dog sitting in a square, ostensibly empty. Just white space. The dog is framed, "separated" from his surroundings, but whether or not the square is "empty" is, as we say in Japan, a matter of interpretation. In fact, it is not empty, but free of obstruction, and the dog seems very attentive to what is happening outside his space. He is listening. And waiting for the burst of song from the white bird perched on the doorway which frames the square in which he sits. Those familiar with the iconography would understand that the bird symbolizes the Spirit which blows when and where it wants.

According to a Dominican legend, St. Jeanne d'Aza, while she was awaiting the birth of the child who became St. Dominic, saw, in a kind of daydream, a dog emerge from her breast carrying a flaming torch in his mouth. In medieval times, with a certain play on words, the Dominicans were called "Domini Canis," dogs of God.

You laugh. You are surprised that we can make jokes about ourselves? Really, the expression is not new. It is found in St. Bernard's writings as long ago as the tenth century.

I'm not laughing at. I'm impressed by the sense of humour. So what does he hear, this bearded dog sitting in the middle of his square?

Human conversation. The conversation of women. Woman, medieval or contemporary, the pious and the profane, have a need to talk, to be listened to. We have both the medieval pious women and the prostitute in this painting. In Picasso's *Les Demoiselles d'Avignon*, les demoiselles were, as we know, the "girls," the prostitutes on the street of Avignon in Barcelona. The dog is listening to the world, to these women outside his circle, remembering his master's injunction "to be in this world and not of this world," always attentive to the mystery expressed at the beginning of time and often symbolized by the humble apple.

Actually, the apple in the painting, dangled by one of the pious women, is for me the most striking part of the canvas. The apple swings like a pendulum, like a measure, in front of shadow figures, oriental silhouettes who are behind *shoji,* opalescent paper windows.

Meaning?

Meaning that the mystery addresses itself equally to the Orient which is still largely unaware of the mystery of salvation.

So these shadow figures dance, unaware, separated from the reality of salvation by this thin paper. Another symbol. Illusion's mask. How does one tear down this mask of illusion, open the doors which bring salvation?

Are my paintings religious? I would say so, but each work lives differently depending on the viewer. It is for you to tell me.

Producing art for a church is a commission. There are both requirements and restrictions. A baptismal font has a job to do, and you are restricted by that, are you not?

No. Challenged, possibly, but not restricted. In fact, my artistic activity is either directly oriented towards a religious production, that is, tied in with a place of prayer, or not. When not, I would say then that the work is for myself. In either case, though, my aim is to express my feelings, the strength of my feelings, not to please anyone. Whether a work is intended for a specific place or not, it is the style of the work which matters. In one way or another, the activity of making art has but one aim: to try to raise earthly truth towards a higher state, "to restore the invisible to the visible."

In that, I would agree with Malraux who said of Goya—this is not an elegant translation, perhaps—"Goya becomes congenial the day he permits himself not to please others, but to please himself in tracking reality, a hidden reality in each of us." I track truth everywhere I can find it.

So your faith and your art have never been in conflict.

In my case I avoid dichotomy. I am tension and dilemma, between earth and sky, sensuality and spirituality, action and thought, art and faith. There is no contest between terrestrial truth, my sensuality, and the sky, my spirituality. One leads to the other. I reconcile the two brothers. Being religious/priest and artist is in a way the same thing. As an artist, I lean equally towards the "Absolute." I am tension between here and eternity. I am the place, the centre, the pivoting point of this meeting. It is the go-between of the yin and the yang of all beings. There are two, but the two are one. It is a way of thinking that brings one back to Hindu philosophy. Without this tension, which is not a conflict for me, there would be no "Life."

The Apple, the Bird and the Parasol: The Collective Unconscious

The apple and the bird are specifically Christian iconography. You have travelled extensively. Have you found a common iconography which straddles cultures and, by extension, religions, since, as you say, religion is determined by culture?

Yes. Many. Everywhere. One example is the canopy, the parasol, or, if you will, the humble umbrella. A very simple form, yet deeply symbolic, and universal. I laboured long to track down the course—parallel courses—of the canopy, which is in its simplest form a stake coming out of the ground, covered, protected by the canopy. Like the hat of a mushroom. Like an umbrella. From another point of view, it is a tree, which is another ancient symbol of great importance, the tree of life. It comes to us today as our Christmas tree. This, the tree of life, we share with many cultures: Chinese, Egyptian, Persian, Mayan, ancient European

The parasol or canopy has been a symbol from the time of the Assyrians and the Egyptians, up to the Roman Catholic procession of "Fête Dieu" of old, a sign of royalty, of divine power. Of the Divinity. In my youth, the priest walked under a canopy during the "Fête Dieu" when he carried the Holy Sacrament in procession. As a religious symbol, the canopy or parasol is still used throughout the world. At Mount Koya in Japan, the headquarters for the Buddhism sect Shingon, I have

In Lingaragh, India with a brahman, 1964.

Gaston, soon after his arrival in Tokyo, spring 1961.

seen monks, high dignitaries in brightly coloured vestments, walk under a parasol. The Ethiopian priests, like the Koya monks, walk under a decorated parasol during religious processions. After the death of the Pontiff in 1978, the Vatican issued two series of postage stamps with the words "sede vacante" and a parasol—in a way, very appropriately—folded. In 1990, on November 12th, to be precise, the Shinto ceremony Sokui-no-Rei, confirmed the rise to the throne of the Japanese Emperor, the Tenno, under a kind of elaborate canopy, the Takamikura.

In the ancient Orient, the canopy was always associated with the reign of the gods: the royal dignitaries who represent themselves as descendants of gods are depicted under a canopy. With the Greeks and the Romans, the canopy indicates the social character of the individual, but with the Indians and the Asians, it underlines divine authority. A drawing and a painting by Delacroix on a trip to Morocco in 1832 shows the Sultan riding a horse in the middle of a crowd. He is followed by a servant holding a parasol above his head.

We can easily follow the development of the symbolic form of the canopy in India, where it goes back very far in history, since the beginning of the Iron Age, tied in one way to burials, strange circular tombs, and in another way with the many levels which crown the Buddha's stupa. In other parts of India, the canopy is associated with branches of the sacred tree, of the "Axis Mundi" from which the sovereign receives his power as "King of the Universe."

Do you want to hear all this?

I think so. Can I decide later?

Yes. But it may be too late. You'll have already heard it. I'll skip to the present. Only a few months ago, there was a program of kabuki theatre on television, a dance called *Kisen, The Joy of Living.* First there was the flowered decor. In ancient Christian iconography, flowers are a sign of joy, the announcment of good news. You will note that I spread flowers in profusion in *The Stunning Message*.

In the midst of this flowered decor, eighty-one-year-old Nakamura Tomijuro dances slowly; his gestures are fairly easy to interpret. Near the end of the dance, his sons, his grandsons, and his great-grandsons join him. A dozen offspring, all dressed like their forebear. It is Children's Day, May 5. They dance with him, around him. Even the littlest one, who is barely two years old, knows how to execute a few steps. You can imagine the pleasure of the crowd at this.

The last tableau is unforgettable. At a signal, they all cluster around the grandfather, except the oldest son, who remains behind his father, holding a huge red parasol above his head. Here, the parasol is a symbol of posterity, of family happiness. The oldest son moves the parasol slowly to the rhythm of small drums and fifes while the small troupe strolls off and disappears behind the big curtain. The beauty of the scene gives you goosebumps.

I have used the parasol in my painting, *The Stunning Message*. On the left side of the canvas, a gentleman is carrying a parasol to a woman on the opposite side of the canvas. She leans towards him graciously. It has the stylization of a kabuki scene. He is handing her the Stunning Message.

The universality of symbols—I can guess, then, that you endorse Jung's concept of the collective unconscious.

My source is not only Jung, although certainly his *Man and His Symbols* was key for me. There is Joseph Campbell's *The Mythic Image*, Marc Girard's *The Symbols in the Bible*, and Othmar Keal's *The Symbols of the Biblical World*.

Let me give you another very clear, indisputable example of the universality of symbols, the Axis Mundi. Humankind has always discovered centres where the divine is strongly palpable, from which a primal energy emanates, centres we call the Axis Mundi or sacred axis. The function of the Axis Mundi is to link the cosmic zones of the universe. The Axis Mundi channels primal energy and so links the three levels: heaven, earth, and underworld. These centres are sometimes marked by an object as simple as a stake or a tree, or one as imposing as a stupa, which starts as a simple mound of earth and becomes an elaborate, squared-off, multi-levelled tower.

Gaston with a Buddhist monk, Bangkok, April 1978.

This axis, which is the supreme manifestation of the sacred, has had different concrete representations. It's Mount Meru of India, Mount Atlas of the Greeks. For Enoch, it was the seventh mountain, the throne of God, the column that holds up the heavens. For Pindar, Mount Etna was a column supporting heaven. It's also the artificial or constructed mountain, the ziggurat. The mountain is the point of juncture of heaven and earth. Located at the middle of the world, it is the image of the world and, by extension, the temple at the summit is part of the mountain. An expanse of the desert permits an encounter with the Absolute, the mountain is the high point favoured by man to attain the Absolute. The mountaintop is the point at which the divinity comes down to meet man; man climbs the mountain to reach the Absolute. It's the meeting place with God. Shiva lives in the upper reaches of the Himalayas. Abraham and Moses were both called up to the mountain to receive their messages from God. The ziggurats, towers—remember the Tower of Babel—and pyramids were built to reach the heavens.

In other words, we recreate the Axis Mundi.

Yes. Definitely. For his religions, man separates, sets aside particular objects, or spaces. Man "creates"—that is to say, raises to the spiritual level—the sacred, his particular sacred object or space. Similar objects and spaces come from a collective unconscious. From mounds which barely rose out of the ground in ancient times, structures were raised which are more and more elaborate, more and more elaborately decorated. Ultimately, temples are constructed. The forms are familiar, and we find these forms everywhere: squares, rectangles, cruciforms, or circles—stupas and domes, ziggurats or pyramids—shapes that we find in Egypt or Central America. In China, this becomes the pagoda, which we also see in some of the Buddhist sites in Japan.

You might tell me that it is the material which dictates it. Perhaps, but those forms also come from the subconscious.

I explored the subject in great depth. Lectured on it. Wrote on it. It has always fascinated me, the extraordinary upsurge of great religious architecture throughout the world in a single period from the eighth to the twelfth century. And this, for me, is possibly the strongest evidence, that in a belt circling the earth between the fifteenth and forty-fifth degrees of latitude, impressive religious structures were built in centuries that seem to have been periods of extraordinary religious fervour and strength, to a point where I could call them Centuries of Faith. You only have to recall a sampling of what has been built in this zone—among the Byôdô-in of Uji in Japan; the Lung-hsing-ssu at Chang-ting-hsien; the numerous multi-level pagodas, the impressively sculpted and painted grottoes of YunKang, Lung-man and Tun-Huang in China; the Angkor complex in Cambodia; the more than 2,000 temples and stupas in the great Pagan Plain of Myanmar; the temples at Orissa, Puri, Madurai, Khajuraho and many others in India; and the gigantic Bamiyan relief sculptures in Afghanistan which, as we all know, were destroyed in March (2001). Add Europe's large number of Roman and Gothic churches; the religious architecture of the Mayans, the Aztecs and other ethnic groups of Central America…

Another more humble example of universality is water. It is a source of life and, what is more humble than this, it cleans. We see water used symbolically as a source of spiritual purification in the majority of religions, in Egyptian religions, in Hinduism, in Shintoism, in Judaism, in Christianity, in Islam.

It is a remarkable phenomenon. The collective subconscious is there and man makes use of it. Religion and its symbols are in the collective subconscious. All it takes is an open mind.

Certainly, for many of us, though, these symbols have lost their meaning.

We have to try to avoid a certain repetition or there is a devaluation. To attract the future generations, we have to create a contemporary iconography, just like Fra Angelico and his peers did when they created a contemporary iconography for their time.

So in effect, if symbols lose their meaning, how a work is viewed changes.

Exactly, and if not viewed at all, a work of art, be it an icon, a sculpture or a simple drawing, is a dead object. It comes to life only when it is looked at, and it comes to life differently depending on the experience of each individual. What will the response of the viewer be tomorrow, next year, or in the next century? Each time the response will be different. The work is never completely finished. It is in constant change because of the fact that it lives only in the eye of the beholder. Da Vinci did not see his *Mona Lisa* in the same way that you or I see it. There are always the cultural appreciation factors of the time to be reckoned with. Never forget that time and culture form or distort appreciation. The Sistine Chapel, seen by contemporaries of Michelangelo, seen before its restoration, and seen now, speaks very different languages. "Shocking," said some of his contemporaries; "prodigious," or "fabulous," said others. And that is also my opinion. Prodigious. Fabulous.

I know I am repeating myself, but I cannot stress this enough: a work of art lives, has a purpose, a value, only through the eyes of the viewer.

You must admit that your use of religious iconography is not obvious. Even your superior did not recognize it.

You have to make an effort to get the meaning. I know that you consider some of my work surrealistic. The surrealists did not have "content" in my sense. I borrow their techniques, perhaps, juxtaposing apparently disparate elements, but the content, the meaning, the intent, differs. With the surrealists, the intent was to break apart traditional ideas of "content."

But I bring to your work my own experiences of time and culture.

Yes. True. I concede. There are certainly other possibilities of understanding and other readings not yet formulated at the unconscious level even by me. Wanting to tell all, reveal all, is neither possible nor desirable. Even if it were possible, an in-depth analysis would not result in a fuller or better understanding of my works and could choke a certain poetry which emanates from it.

Honesty vs. Curiosity: The Study of Buddhism

There are many visual references to Buddhism in your work. How did you come to study Buddhism?

At first, more by honesty than by curiosity, or vice versa, I'm not sure which. I tried to understand what Siddhartha Gautama brought to the world when he became Buddha. Buddha—Buddhism—has had an enormous influence on the cultures of the world. I had come to live in a Buddhist country. I needed to understand this influence, so I tried to understand the basic ideas, the themes, and to put these in parallel with Jesus's words. For instance, compassion, from the Latin *compassio,* to feel with, to be with, to sympathize with, to fall in parallel with. In Buddhism the idea of "compassion" literally means "to agree with," "to be compatible with," "to share the troubles of another." We see this in the wonderful stories in the Jatakas. The Jatakas are a collection of 537 legends about the past births of the Buddha. In one of these stories, the

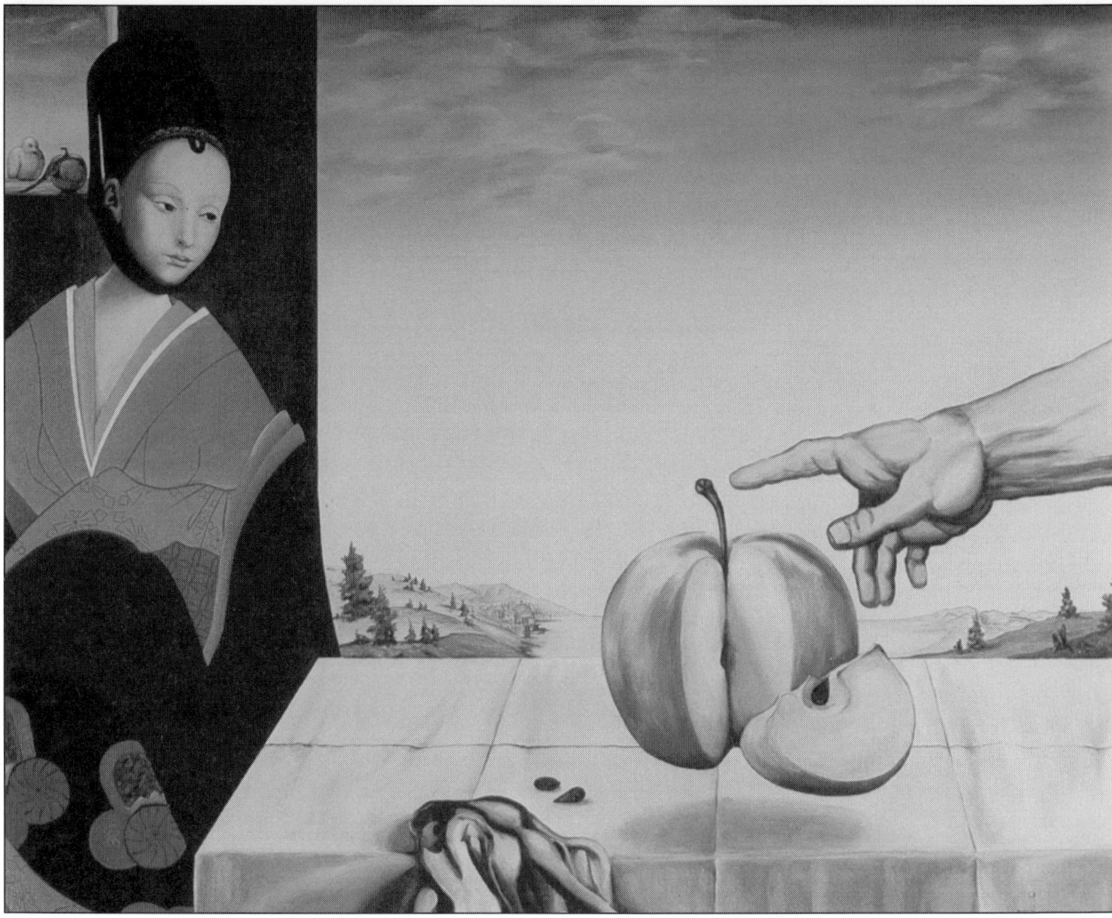

Window for Suspended Fruit, painting on canvas, 1981.

Buddha sees a tiger who doesn't have enough food to feed her young. The Buddha is so overcome by compassion that he throws himself into the tiger's path.

What we often forget is that Jesus had the same grand compassion, to the extent that he gave himself, his life, as "saviour of the world." Mind you, in teachings about Jesus, compassion is usually interpreted or translated as charity, a translation of less depth, I think.

Theologically speaking, I find Hinduism much richer than Buddhism because it is centred on the concept of the triad, Vishnu, Brahma, and Shiva. Are they three gods or one god? Are they three gods, three abilities, or three manifestations of one and the same god? Hindu theologians would say that these entities are interchangeable, that they are three aspects of the same entity which manifests itself in the creation, the sustaining, and the destruction of the cosmos.

When I studied Hinduism more deeply, I understood that for Hindus the existential experience of the world is the basis of this formulation, this way of thinking. First there is Creation: something appears, something happens. Then things "are," they remain in existence: they change, this is the maintenance of the cosmos. Finally, there is disintegration, destruction, death. One could postulate that out of this existential experience, the concept of the triad Vishnu, Brahma, and Shiva was born. At the core of this thinking, of course, is human experience. In creation, something happened, so we are alive; things exist, so there is maintenance; finally there is death, destruction. I assume that the three aspects of god, or of the one god, developed from this cyclic experience.

Christianity and Hinduism have enveloped the concept of "creation" in extraordinary imagery—fabulous and wonderful in the etymological sense of the words, what strikes the spirit.

But the interpretation of creation is very different. In the Judeo-Christian-Muslim tradition, creation takes place over seven days.

The Hindu version of creation is no less marvellous. I'll give you a very simplified Vishnu version—and you will see that the two essential elements in the practice of the Hindu religion appear here: meditation and austerity. Vishnu, stretched out on Anata, the many-headed cobra, floats infinite and immobile on an ocean of milk, the *om*. From Vishnu's navel rises the life force, the pink lotus flower upon which sits the first aspect of the Divine, here playing a concrete role, that of the creator Brahma, or the Primordial Ancestor. He has four arms, each of which holds a book, and four mouths, each of which recites one of these books. These are the Vedas. The laws laid down in these books were not enough for the Creator. He needed to understand their origin and their purpose as well as his own reason for existing. He went down into the stem of the lotus, but his search was in vain; he found nothing. So he began to meditate. Vishnu appeared to him, blessed him and ordered him to give himself over to fiery austerity. Only the heat that he engendered would allow him to proceed to creation.

Let's take the concept of creation which recurs frequently in Hinduism and place it in parallel with the concept of creation as we find it in the Bible. In Hinduism creation means re-formation of matter which is and always will be: the cosmos has always replaced itself and always will. For those who believe in the Bible, Creation is an actualization "from nothing." Ex nihilo. This would be the initial "Big Bang." And the cosmos proceeds to a final absolute, "the end of the world." The fabulous aspect of Hinduism goes beyond this concept. The Hindu concept of creation is that after eons and eons of time, everything goes flat, becomes "formless." Vishnu sleeps on the sea of eternity. From his navel sprouts a lotus flower on which sits Brahma, the new breath of life, and everything starts again. Beautiful, fabulous images.

You seem so fascinated—or impressed—by Hinduism, I'm surprised that you didn't jump ship.

No need. The study of other religions has helped me understand my own spiritual and theological concepts better. It has deepened my faith. This is an attitude which has been increasingly adopted in the Christian milieu, by the way. This is Ecumenism, dialogue with other kinds of religious thinking. I do not blur the border. This is not syncretism. Syncretism is too easy. Parallelism with a clear mind is more honest. But in the end it is a question of faith. You either believe with an awakened, enlightened mind in a Book, the Bible, or not.

I believe in my religion, but I do not deny others their religions. I start with the principle that God creates all men. How does man answer, communicate, turn towards Him? Some try to do it, some don't, and still others refuse to do it. Some believe in a notion called revelation. The Judeo-Christian tradition is based on a revelation. Let's say this is a supplementary way to attune to Him. To the Christian believer, it is a surer way to attain what one is looking for.

But I do not say that there is no truth outside the Judeo-Christian revelation. This is false. As a being created by God, every man has some means to become attuned to Him. Man naturally has some truth within himself. The old saying *hors de l'église point de salut,* outside of the church there is no salvation, was scratched from Roman Catholic teaching a long time ago. So was the concept of Hell as a place. It is not. It is a situation in which one is deprived of a return to the Principal—who is a Person according to revelation—that created me.

So you are arguing for universality in belief as well as in the universality of artistic images.

I'll give you another example. In the 1970s, thirty of us were invited to Sophia University to meet the Dalai Lama. He was an extremely engaging personality, with a great simplicity, and a great warmth. He talked with us for almost an hour. One point in particular has stayed with me. He said something to the effect of, "Let's put all our philosophies, all our beliefs aside. Whether there is one God or not, what are we left with? Me, not much, a being and on the other side, a great whole of which I am also a part. All I can do is place myself before the great whole, like a figure praying before the Absolute."

I thought about these words for a long time. I found an echo of them in Father Geffré, a Dominican, who stated that even if there exist—and will always exist—doctrinal differences which separate us, the followers of the great religions, the meeting point which unites us or the note that we sound in tune "is an equal dynamism of the spiritual order when it concerns the meeting of man and the absolute." The Dalai Lama's point about being part of a great whole, Father Geffré states differently, possibly not so simply: "It is something which turns always around a decentring of self for the sake of another centre—whether this centre is defined as God or as the absolute, or as Supreme Reality." I believe this is what the Dalai Lama was trying to tell us, in different words.

Every true religion aims at establishing a link between the adept and the Absolute. I'm not speaking of a cult. When the faithful of whatever religion is honestly trying to establish that link, he answers to the truth within him. He does not accept that he is merely a material being, just so much matter. He goes beyond. He also sees himself as a spiritual being. This ongoing, living truth can, however, be revised, enriched, developed. It's the same thing for someone who says he follows no path at all. He has his own thoughts about his existence, his conscience. Man is not simply pure spirit. He also has a body and he is a social animal. He needs symbols, rites, credos, precepts, etc. He creates them according to his needs.

This is the teaching of Roman Catholicism. And it is also mine. It would take a book to fully explain this point. I will stop here.

Hinduism and Krishnamurti

What was the "click," if I can borrow one of your artistic terms, that brought you to the study of Hinduism?

The interest developed over time. I first studied Hinduism briefly while I was studying Asian

Mr. Murti, Gaston Petit and Krishnamurti in Madras, India, 1981.

cultures at university not long after I arrived in Japan, which was in the early 1960s. Then in 1981 I had a very moving experience in Madras, India, when I spent some time there with a couple of Hindus. Mr. Murti, the master of the house, was a specialist in the very ancient and sacred texts, the Vedas. His brother, Mr. Krishnamurti, you know as the famous poet. They were both intellectuals and deeply religious. They knew that I was a Dominican priest, and Mr. Krishnamurti had been thoughtful and considerate enough to read up on the life of St. Dominic and St. Catherina of Sienna, the Dominican mystic. He recalled snippets of their lives during our conversation, long conversations, which lasted many hours. I was very touched. They asked me many questions about God, the Soul, the Bible, the story of Creation and how it was interpreted, about Noah and the Flood, the bloody conquests of David, the great epics of the Old Testament, about Christianity, Jesus, His divinity, His resurrection, the teachings of the Church… I in turn had many questions about their myths; their religious devotions; about the idea of Brahma as the ultimate reality; the Vedic hymns, the Vedas, which are like very dense summaries; the many gods and their attributes; the idea of creation; universal destruction; the transmigration of souls.

That was when I was profoundly struck by how other people could live fully a faith different from my own. For the Hindu, any relationship established with a transcendent being can be called a religion. Hinduism does not know heresy because it is a rainbow, as varied as its sacred books, which are so numerous that it is impossible to read them all.

I cannot but have the greatest respect for people who live with such conviction while at the same time remaining open to the seeking of other spiritual experiences, other concepts of the cosmos.

Each and every one of us is seeking spirituality, a world which is beyond us. We all crave the Absolute.

After my visit with the Murtis, I took a good week on the island of Bali, a kind of retreat. Walking the beaches, I digested everything I had just learned and experienced. I had lived for fifty years according to the teachings of the Bible, which for me contain the word of God revealed. Through revelation God spoke to mankind—and continues to speak. He made me, a being / an individual / a person, and continues to make me because creation isn't simply an act of the past: God sustains my existence. Because I am created as a being / an individual / a person, I am me, solely responsible for my actions towards He that created me. I must answer to his Word. He calls me to Him. This direct and permanent bond between my Creator and me distances me forever from reincarnation.

My friends in Madras do not have Revelation. Their thinking, no matter how deep and lucid, can never lead them to this. The cyclical nature of the world leads them irreducibly to the "eternal return" of being, both spiritual, the soul, and physical, material. In this perspective reincarnation is an integral part of the structure. They cannot escape it.

My fascination with their world that is so distant, so different and sometimes so deep, has affected me to this day.

Original Sin: The Vertigo of Virtue

Do you research Christianity with the same intensity as you have researched other religions?

Yes, absolutely. This is also a way to nourish my faith and keep it alive. It is important to be reminded that this is a living religion. We are not static. If there was change in the past, is it not possible, perhaps even necessary, in the present?

There is a brilliant book by Elaine Pagels, *Adam, Eve and the Serpent,* which describes the evolution of Christian attitudes toward morality from the time of Jesus to that of Augustine. At the core of the book is the examination of what came to be called "original sin."

Before the fourth century, Genesis 1-3 was interpreted as an affirmation of human freedom and the ability of man to choose between good and evil. Pagels has a chapter, "Christians Against the Roman Order," which studies the social context of the time. Christianity meant liberation, a freedom to worship Christ rather than the rulers of this world, and it became known as a religion of emancipation. Christianity exhibited freedom in the face of idolatry and all types of oracles, while at the same time offering a rational understanding of the universe and the moral world; this was the point of view of Clement of Alexandria of Origene and the Church Fathers in general. For many of the early leaders of the early church, freedom was the practical message of the gospel.

In the fourth century, a different point of view emerged. August of Hippo, the theologian who was to become St. Augustine, found Genesis 1-3 to be an affirmation of universal bondage to sin, and his argument prevailed. Although originally a champion of free will, he went on to pursue a study of Genesis which was aimed at destroying Manichaeism—Donatians and Pelagians, as well—with arguments based on the consequences of the Fall. His conclusion was that it was a story of human bondage. St. Augustine's interpretation became the doctrine of the church, not without heavy debate, mind you, which went on even after his death in 430.

In fact, it was Augustine who saw in Genesis 1-3 the connection between universal servitude and sin.

I also study man, which is of course also a study of the self. My study of the collective unconscious has not been related solely to art. The idea of the collective unconscious takes one deep into oneself. Jung was very new for me. The result of my French Canadian education was my belief that the subconscious as non-rational had to be sublimated, if not repressed. Freud with all his talk of libido was dangerously suspicious. Jung was more acceptable. From Jung I learned that man cannot fully realize himself—and this relates to man and his religions— if he does not have a full understanding of himself through his dreams and his symbols. So I devised a way to jot down dreams in the dark whenever I woke up. Mind you, I usually fell back asleep with the pencil in my hand. The following morning, I would try to decipher these scribbles and sort them out as best I could. I discovered a pattern, a recurrent dream which I recognized as a message. As you know, each "code" is individual. I know mine. I still have that "personal" loose-leaf notebook which I can show you—and show only!

"Show" only. I'm sure you don't mind if I express disappointment.

Before we go on—we're talking about the popular concept of sin, the snake, the apple—was the fruit in question actually an apple? It seems to me that the apple is a rather modern fruit, and certainly a fruit of the temperate climates of the northern hemisphere.

No. Let me set the record straight. Obviously it was not an apple. This legendary designation comes from a phonetic shortcut: in the Vulgate, the Latin Bible established by Saint Jerome, the word "fruit" is translated as *pomum.* As far as the tree goes, "knowledge" contains no sexual connotation, either. Shame on Philon of Alexandria, who was the first to see the forbidden fruit as sex. Shame on St. Augustine, too, for whom the couple was shocked and ashamed by their nudity—their sexuality—for having eaten the forbidden fruit and for whom the transgression would be perpetuated henceforth by sexuality *ad aeternum.*

Original sin is defined solely by the penchant of man to take himself for a god. Alphonse Maillot in *Eve, ma mère, Eve, My Mother,* sums it up thus: It certainly wasn't to do wrong that Eve wanted to take the fruit, but to know how to do good at all times. The tree was the tree of knowledge. She dreamed of becoming infallible on an ethical level. The fall was not an orgy, but a lying intelligence, that of the snake, hidden beneath desire combined with virtue and immortality. Eve felt the vertigo of virtue. Eve sought to transform virtue into a gift. It was by the grace of God that the knowledge of good and evil came, not as a result of a failure of the human spirit.

St. Augustine's interpretation did society no service. Pagels states it very succinctly—are we allowed to quote in an interview?

Yes, but we have to say who said it.

I quote. Pagels: "By insisting that humanity, ravaged by sin, now lies helplessly in need of outside intervention, Augustine's theory could not only validate secular power but justify as well the imposition of church authority, by force, if necessary, as essential for human salvation."

You said "shame on"—do you see change coming in the twenty-first century? Do you think it's possible to revise or at least to balance the Augustine position of the fourth century?

Certainly, the question is open—to many like me. Secular power no longer needs the validation of the church. The social context of the twentieth century has brought radical changes. People have become more aware of their human responsibility and freedom. Today, we are witnessing a revolution in social attitudes regarding sexuality, politics, and religion.

What kind of change would you foresee then? Can you give me an example?

One example—we are talking about the concept of sin. Couldn't baptism, then, which has been regarded solely as an act to "erase" original sin, also have another significance? Jesus received baptism from John the Baptist. Did he need to be erased of original sin? Or could baptism be a symbol of being accepted as "a child of God," i.e., becoming a member of the people of God, a member of a community which expresses its alliance to God?

Other books study specific aspects of Christianity. *Jésus de Nazareth* by Heinz Zahrnt tries to bring Jesus closer to mankind. He lived in his social environment just as you and I live in ours. *Credo* by Hans Küng explains, in a simple way, sayings which have been repeated for over 1,500 years and still have meaning for us today. I think, though, that this book is more for Christians than non-Christians. *The Meaning of Jesus: Two Visions* by Marcus J. Borg and N.T. Wright aims at giving us a definitive image on the historical Jesus. People think that the Bible is the story of Jesus's life. It is not. The gospels are not biographies of Jesus. Everything in the Bible is arranged as a teaching. We know very little about Jesus's life. We know only that at the age of seven, he was spending a great deal of time at the Temple, that he was questioning the rabbis who were, effectively, the doctors of theology for their time, and that he was very bright, very precocious.

About his life between the ages of seven and thirty, we know absolutely nothing. The Four Gospels were intended to teach. They are not about the life of Jesus at all.

Paris, Existentialism, and La Grande Sartreuse

What about this wonderful very Beat photo of you in a black turtleneck and black pants when you were in Paris?

I have had the good fortune to be in many places at the right time. Paris at the beginning of the sixties, the golden years of existentialism, for instance. I was plunged into the movement. Jean-Paul Sartre was the high priest and Simone de Beauvoir the high priestess—referred to informally as La Grande Sartreuse. They had thousands and thousands of followers. You can see by my photograph—I am in black; I have long hair and a goatee; I am very serious in the existentialist style. I felt an affinity. I had taken a course in existentialism during my studies in the fifties. But delving deeper, I realized that the path wasn't open. Existentialism was blocked at a death-birth nihilism. Its nihilism went against my deepest convictions. In the end I came to prefer the vision of Camus over the jargon and nihilistic approach of Sartre.

So you completely abandoned existentialism.

Not completely. Eventually, I came across Colin Wilson's book *The Outsider.* For me, Wilson gives existentialism new life. He creates an existentialism which isn't paralyzed by its own nihilism. In another book, his *Introduction to New Existentialism,* he covers existentialism beginning with Kierkegaard, managing to pin down the weak points which lead to the impasse of nihilism. His thesis is that when these falsehoods are circumvented, existentialism can become one of the most powerful instruments of human intelligence, an intellectual adventure which could perfectly control human existence.

How do you integrate your religious convictions with this flirtation with existentialism?

Gaston in Tokyo, 1978.

Religion or the religious act isn't a simple experience. As Louis Dupré explains so well in *The Other Dimension*, the religious act is of another dimension. The spirit discovers a new reality.

Which I presume must be integrated with the reality of the quotidian, of the world of the five senses.

Yes. In my case, it has been by looking into other religions, especially Hinduism, that I've understood that my own personal search is to attain, discover, seize, apprehend—words fail—the Reality which integrates all realities. I'd say that this search is the basis of all religions. It's this search which made me both understand and accept the truth of others...

You're not going to put all this in, are you?

Why not?

This is information just for you. No one is interested in the history of original sin or my research into Jung.

I would argue that the breadth of a man's interests and the depth of his knowledge are relevant to our understanding of his complexity.

Let me go back to something you said earlier. You use the word "preach" in the sense of "teach."

Yes, absolutely. The Dominican motto is "To search for the truth in order to give the truth." This dates from the time of St. Thomas Aquinas (1225-1274), an outstanding Dominican, philosopher and theologian. This was fundamental to his teaching. In fact, it formed the basis of thirteenth-century scholasticism and became the official teaching of the church. The Dominicans are very conscious of this, that the search is essentially linked to giving. This constitutes our sense of identity.

The Dominican Order allows, in fact, demands, the equilibrium between meditation and action. There is no "meaning" to a Dominican who does not go into action, as there is no "meaning" to a Dominican who does not meditate. Dominic insisted that his brothers live "in" this world, close to universities.

One must consider the landscape of his time in thirteenth-century Europe. Europe was still heavily forested, although there were a few cities with universities. There were a number of abbeys located in the forests. Contemplative monks lived in remote abbeys "out" of this world. St. Dominic wanted his followers to pursue a dual purpose, a dual life; a contemplative and an active life. The equilibrium is all-important. The Franciscan Order was formed in the same century, but the focus was entirely different. St. Francis came from the upper class, and he was revolting against materialism, so he formed an order which would live in poverty. Education became important to Franciscans much later.

Here in Shibuya we live in a community, a convent, but each of us has our own work. One takes care of the parish here; another teaches philosophy at Tokyo University; another helps other parishes in Tokyo; three who are not ordained brothers help to take care of the house. We contemplate in order to give to others the fruit of contemplation. It is in this sense that we "spread the truth." So one cannot be self-centred.

I prefer "convent" to "monastery," by the way. "Monastery" refers to the living habitation of monks. "Convent" comes from the Latin *conventus,* which means "assembly." It applies to habitations of both men and women.

One of the characteristics of the Dominican Order is that one is encouraged to make one's own way in accordance to one's own gifts and talents. I am not the first artist. Fra Angelico (1387-1455) was a Dominican. Father Couturier, another Dominican, was a friend of many of the most important artists in France before the war—Picasso, Rouault, Matisse, Chagall; Father Kim, a Korean; Father Carpentier, a Belgian; Fathers Regamey and Cocagnac initiated the art magazine *L'Art sacré.* It was Father Regamey who inspired Le Corbusier to build the Dominican convent at l'Arbrelle in France. It was also Father Regamey who influenced the delightful, very unique chapel in Assy which was illustrated by many of the great artists of the time: Rouault, Matisse, and Richier, as well as Léger, who was, by the way, an atheist. They were all invited by Father Regamey to contribute.

Death

You talk of absolutes, the absolute. Most religions talk about the hereafter, Nirvana, Paradise. Life as we know it, no matter what we believe, has an end. We call that death. Are you afraid of death?

I don't like the word "death." We've used it so much, ridiculed it even, worn it out. It has a quaint macabre sense. I much prefer "end of the journey," "passage" or even "transition."

Yes, I have thought about this end of the journey, especially the day my doctor told me, "The biopsy of the tissue sample is positive." Cancer. Suddenly I saw the sword of Damocles balanced above my head. I have a lot of energy, but my health has never been extraordinary. I have had many illnesses which required serious surgical intervention, the first when I was only about ten years old to deal with my hearing problem. I've been anaesthetized more than half a dozen times. And that's not mentioning the other illnesses everyone suffers from, like allergies to pollen, sumac (which in Canada is called poison ivy), shiitake mushrooms, which some people can eat but which are disastrous for me.

I have never heard you complain about illness; the only illness I have been aware of was your concern about cancer, and even then, it seemed to be more like scientific interest. I seem to remember you asking the surgeon if you could be allowed to somehow watch your own surgery.

I wanted to see what was going on.

I did have an odd experience in the fall of 2000, related not to health, but to death. It had to do with incense.

Incense?

I had been invited to celebrate mass in a parish in the heart of Paris. Right at the beginning of the mass as the thurifer passed, I was enveloped in incense. Suddenly, I was "other." I felt beyond the grave.

That's interesting—now that you mention it, I have never noticed incense in your studio.

I use incense very rarely. Incense has a very specific meaning in Japan. It is used as a fragrance—there is even an incense ceremony, much like the tea ceremony. You inhale the smoke and try to identify which rare and expensive wood essence the fragrance comes from. But as you know, incense is also widely used here in Japan for funeral ceremonies. It is never used during eucharistic celebrations as it is in the West. I say funeral ceremonies because in Japan people are cremated after death, so it is a ceremony rather than a funeral.

This might be a non sequitur, but we know that all religions use candles. And tonight I see fourteen, two times your magic number seven, glowing in every corner of your studio.

They are a kind of meditation for me. A thought which is at the same time a lesson. The flame flickers and sparkles. The oil or the wax is consumed. When I blow out the candle, where does the flame go? For the Buddhist, man is like a lit candle. When he stops breathing, where does he go, what remains?

I'm sorry. I've sidetracked you from the original question: are you afraid of death?

Nyes. You know what I mean—yes and no. I'd say yes because I must face the unknown, the unknowable absolute. No one returns to tell us what it is. But "no" in tiny letters because maybe, when I reason with myself... Is there no possibility of escaping this cutting-off, this break? The question remains, what is there after this life? When my flame goes out, what does it become, where does it go? Various cultures have created a paradise after this life. Beautiful images. A paradise of a place? I don't think so. A way of being "other"? Perhaps. I wouldn't be surprised...although how could I be surprised if I didn't exist any more, if this "other" didn't even exist in God, who is completely "another."

At the same time, I am not really convinced that the game ends with death—so we come to the "n" of "nyes"—because I believe that an Absolute exists, an Absolute to which we terrestrial beings give specific personal characteristics and which we like to define by quite precise criteria, which raises a question to which I do not have an answer. Why do these particular chromosomes, out of thousands produced at the moment of conception, one particular sperm and one particular egg, come into contact to make "me"? Why me and not another?

I believe in God the creator, regardless of the name we give Him, and it is He who has made it happen like this, so that I am speaking these words and not another. Whether it is this specific act of my arrival in this world He made happen, or whether I am simply part of the whole cosmic development, I cannot say. Mysterious indeed.

For me, that I am this combination of chromosomes with my consciousness, means nothing more than chaos. Chance.

My response is that it is in the plan of God. It is a plan that he sets in motion. Everything is in the act of creation. It is organized creation. Even if it is a plan, for me, it is difficult to go as far as saying that God puts his nose in every little thing. It is not impossible, but it is useless. He sets the laws in motion, and knows everything will happen, knows I will come, you will come. We think in time, but there is no time for Him. For God, time does not exist. He is outside time. He created time and space at the same time.

I would not go so far as the kabbalists, the Jewish mystics, to say that God created the creative causes of the world, but doesn't especially look after the world. He does look after it. One of the great underlying problems is time; a phenomenon that exists only for us. We live in time. For God there is no time. He is simply everything. Perhaps the most important thing for human beings is the feat of having existed, or having been able to love, of having been able to help some fellow creatures to love more, too. Maybe this is "paradise," maybe it is here. Love. Help. Share. When one knows the profound meaning of those words.

III

JAPAN: A JUMP INTO THE UNKNOWN

Gaston Petit arrived in Tokyo during the post-war reconstruction of the early sixties, a very different city from the high-rise and neon glitz that is Tokyo today. Petit's artistic career took off almost as soon as he arrived. Studies in Japanese calligraphy led to a complete shift in his artistic style to the abstract, finding expression in his stained glass windows, paintings and lithographs. Production in his printing studio led to teaching: some of Japan's major artists in lithography began their careers working with Petit.

Japan, a jump into the unknown, imbues his work.

What were your first impressions of Japan?

Darkness. Not dark, but darkness. I landed at night at Haneda. There were very few flashy billboards like we see today, no painted buildings along the road like I was used to in Canada, yellow, green and red painted balconies, red brick houses. Coming from the airport was depressing. I had the impression that the air was filled with a languorous sadness, maybe a result of the war. This was scarcely fifteen years after the war—fourteen, to be precise. Tokyo had been devastated by the bombing and the fires. Almost no buildings had been left standing. I won't mention the harshness of the language which I set about learning the next day, alone with a teacher who couldn't speak a word of any other single language.

There was a titanic effort to finish the facilities for the Olympics and the 246 highway. So around Shibuya station, it was a real mess. I used to need to wear rubber boots to walk to the station from here. There was only one ten-story building along that street, and now there are tall buildings on both sides of the street that form a flat wall ten stories high—crowned by a forty-story building being built as we speak.

The only way to go to Aoyama was through the Dogenzaka—there was a tramway with charming bells. There were night *udon*, noodle wagons, and beer stalls around Shibuya station, replaced by a bus terminal today, and of course many fewer cars. A sort of odd-looking three-wheeled half-motorcycle vehicle, dark brown, was omnipresent.

The Japan I came to in 1961 was still rather shabby. The materials available for art and construction were, in general, poor quality. You could find foreign foods and foreign goods—mostly American—in a few places. Clothes weren't good quality, and usually were too small for me. The Japanese were much smaller then. When I stood on the trains, I could see over most heads. Not today. People would glare at you as if you were an alien. Often when you spoke to someone in Japanese, they would reply without even listening: *Eigo ga wakarimasen.* "I don't understand English."

On the other hand, at times, after lunch, I would go for a walk and drop into a *kissaten* not only for the excellent coffee, but to listen to people talking, to ask questions. It was also a way to practice Japanese. People were very kind, very appreciative of the fact that I was making an effort to learn their language.

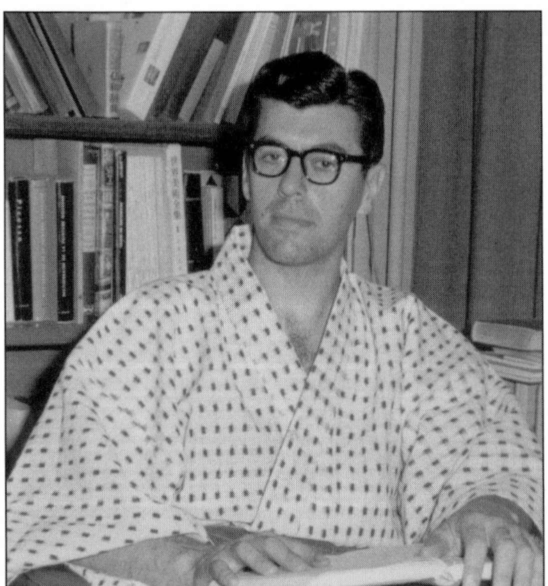

Gaston in study corner, Tokyo, summer 1961.

***Kissaten*? Forty years ago? When I was coming here only six years ago, I was worried about coffee deprivation. And was amazed to find excellent coffee almost everywhere. But surely forty years ago, Japan was still the land of tea.**

No, it was the same forty years ago. There were coffee shops, *kissaten*, all over the place. In fact, for me, the *kissaten* were an education in good coffee. Trois-Rivières is full of coffee shops today, but then, there was not one. Coffee was what they offered you with your dinner or your lunch, wash water, actually. Very light coffee, or over-cooked perked coffee. Although my father liked really good coffee, so he bought—I remember the name—Bokar coffee—very good, and strong, and perked, but served fresh.

But these were only first reactions. There was much that was very exciting. Japan fostered my artistic development. It began immediately. When I arrived, our church was celebrating the first anniversary. The windows were in, but they were in clear glass, hence my assignment to design 1000 square feet of stained glass windows.

You have said that coming to Japan was "a jump into the unknown." How do you think living in Japan has affected Gaston Petit, the person?

Of course, the person is not separate from the artist. I have learned in Japan an attention to detail; I have learned patience; and I have developed my ability to adapt. I did not like fish before coming to Japan. Now I love it, even raw. I love the Japanese space and materials, the wood, the straw, the paper. I sleep on a futon in my tatami room. In the morning, I fold it up and put it away, and as you see, it is a day room. We never wear shoes in this room. A person's way of being, sitting, even sleeping in this room are different. I do calligraphy on handmade paper in this room. I have developed a sensitivity coloured by my life in Japan. From my experience here I've concluded that one's milieu forms and transforms an individual: his personality, his choices, his expectations.

So I am aware now of having many different layers. Japan has made me more discerning. It has helped me understand myself better: who I am, where I stand, what values I wish to preserve, what choices I must make, what is purely a cultural envelope and can be discarded. Every adult has to be discriminating within his own culture, but here this sense becomes more acute, this awareness of being a Westerner, and of behaviour which comes from living in a Japanese society.

Of course, the adjustment is not perfect. If I like the unwritten rules of not spelling out every word in a conversation—intuition supplements—at times my logical Western education results in my feeling highly frustrated. One must use two different ways to communicate: with a Westerner, one is more direct, and with the Japanese, more meandering. I have to switch from one to the other all the time. Just like switching cassettes.

If I had remained in Canada, I would surely not have followed the same path, covered the same ground. By nature I am tolerant, I think, but I was forced to become more tolerant by accepting my daily frustrations—the never going directly to the point, my lack of vocabulary. Of course, language isn't everything. Without knowing all the nuances of a language, even a minimum sometimes suffices, along with human warmth, to be understood and to make good, even indispensable friends. But it must be said, we remain outsiders. Living in a community like Shibuya composed of Japanese and foreigners—Poles, Spaniards—has dulled the effects of the Seidensticker Syndrome, as they say here, the syndrome of a foreigner loving Japan, then hating it, and finally recovering his love for the country.

An analogy I use is that the Japanese themselves encircle us in a kind of garden. Forty years ago, this was absolutely the way to be. Foreigners are more widely accepted today, but I would say that this is still true. One is totally at home within this garden, but beware if you want to cross the border. I know my borders, and I am happy. I am totally at ease in what I consider my garden. I love so many aspects of Japanese culture, yet I have a strong sense of not being Japanese. Intense studies in my first years helped me understand more about this culture, but it is impossible to be so immersed in this society as to feel fully at home.

Why do you think that is?

The most obvious problem is language, which is and will always be, a problem for foreigners, unless you are born, brought up and educated in Japan. If you ask me what the difficulty is, the poverty is, I'd have to say it's expressing myself in the country where I have spent half my life. I have to work with a vocabulary that often fails me—although others consider me fluent in Japanese. In general, no matter how fluent you are, there is twenty per cent or more of the language that you will never master, and that is the *Tennô* language, the levels of politeness. The levels of politeness include the children's language, women's language, men's language, language if you are speaking to someone moderately superior, or very superior, or to an equal; language with an inferior, but again, there are many levels: moderately inferior, very inferior… There are more than twenty ways to say hello, depending on to whom one is speaking. Less dangerous, but possibly as frustrating, is the counting system. The counting system changes depending on whether you are counting the number of persons, the number of houses, the number of ships, the number of cars, the number of pencils, the number of sheets of paper, the days of the month, the number of days—There are more than thirty counting systems. "One" is *ichi*; the first day of the month is *tsuitachi;* one piece of paper is *ichimai*; one bottle is *ippon*; one person is *hitori*… You get my point, I think. St. Francis Xavier once said, "It is the language of the devil."

What brought you to Japan? Surely it is a long way from a convent in Ottawa to Tokyo.

Not so far, in fact. Every Dominican province or "group" has one or a couple of fields of mission. Japan has been Canada's field of mission since 1927, so I met missionaries coming back on sabbatical and young Japanese Dominicans coming to our House of Studies in Ottawa, which is now a university, to pursue their studies. The present, and rather ill, Japanese bishop of Sendai was a classmate of mine, Monsignor Raymond Chihiro Sato. He was ordained in Ottawa the same day as I was, April 3, 1959. I had given my life to God and the Order. To preach/teach in Canada or Japan made no difference to me. On my ordination day, I asked to come to Japan. I was delighted when my superior said yes, and I have never regretted my choice.

The charge of a Dominican is to "communicate to others the fruit of one's contemplation." Preaching, teaching in all its forms, even through art, is communicating the fruit of one's contemplation.

Allow me to simply quote you a passage from St. Paul. Do you want the citation for this as well? I Corinthians, 12:4-11 "Now there are diversities of gifts, but the same Spirit. And there are differences of administrations, but the same Lord. And there are diversities of operations, but it is the same God which worketh all in all. But the manifestation of the Spirit is given to every man to profit withal. For to one is given by the Spirit the word of wisdom; to another the word of knowledge by the same Spirit; To another the working of miracles; to another prophecy; to another discerning of spirits; to another divers kinds of tongues; to another the interpretation of tongues: But all these worketh that one and the selfsame Spirit, dividing to every man severally as he will."

Japan is usually thought of as an entirely Buddhist country. Your Catholic church at Shibuya holds five or six hundred people. I was surprised that at the service I attended, there were very few non-Japanese. I had assumed that the church would be primarily for foreigners temporarily living in Japan, as is the case with the synagogue in Tokyo. Are most of your congregation Japanese?

Yes, they are, and our services are entirely in Japanese. We have a very active membership, in fact, and they come from as far as Yokohama, which can be a good hour by car. Missionaries first came to Japan in 1549 when Francis Xavier arrived on the island of southern Kyhushu. Converts are said to have reached 300,000 by the end of the century.

Shintoism, the traditional religion of Japan, is animistic with, some say, as many as 800 gods which have specific functions, a god to whom one prays for good business, another god—and another temple—to whom one prays to pass entrance exams, and so on. I've read that one reason that Christianity was so easily accepted was that Jesus was considered, at least at first, as one more god along with all the rest.

That may be so. Under the Tokugawa shogunate in the early seventeeth century (1603-1867), Christianity was considered a threat—as was Buddhism, actually. Christianity was proscribed, foreigners were forbidden to enter the country, and the church was all but extinguished. Because of internal conflicts many Buddhist temples were destroyed and monks were put to death as well.

One of the tests, I understand, was to be required to step on the cross. If there was hesitation—guilty. Thousands of the Japanese Christians were martyred.

Yes, and from this time, the so-called Kakure Kristian, hidden Christians, secretly practiced their religion for over two centuries, just like the hidden Jews in Spain after the Spanish Inquisition.

In 1865 a group of people at Nagasaki publicly identified themselves as Christians, and then other communities of Kakure Kristian were discovered in the region, as many as 60,000 people. They were in remote areas where government surveillance was at its weakest. But of these 60,000, only half chose to return to their reintroduced religion. Not surprising, perhaps: the anti-Christian laws were still in effect then, and many of the discovered Christians were jailed or exiled to other parts of the country.

Among the hidden Jews, some of the rituals changed over time.

This was also the case with the Kakure Kristian. They had preserved their faith, but in many cases ritual practices had mixed with Shintoism or Buddhism, so they were far from being orthodox.

Six or seven years ago, a very old woman who lived not far from our church here across from the Philippine Embassy passed away. Her son came to ask for a Christian funeral. His mother had been a Kakure Kristian. We had never met her; she had never come to church. Since then, both the son and his wife have received baptism. Many of our congregation are converts, but a number come from generations of Catholicism that was practiced in hiding.

Except for your stints practicing calligraphy in a fishing village in Ibaraki prefecture for a summer, you have lived continually in Shibuya.

Yes, always at the same address. Living here the entire time has given me the unique opportunity to observe. And to be part of the community. One of my favourite restaurants, for instance, is an Italian restaurant. The owner came from Italy during the war as a sailor, developed a taste for his own *calamari*, married a Japanese woman, had three sons, and today his sons each have a highly successful restaurant. As far as I know, although he is in his eighties now, in Italian fashion, father still dictates the recipes. We have grown old together, I would say.

Should I point out for our readers that Shibuya is one of the most desirable addresses in Tokyo?

Yes, now. Not then. It was rather quiet then, and old. Look at the old wooden home/shop across the street from me. What you see now are the high fashion boutiques, and classy, expensive restaurants surrounding this very old, humble home. This street, the Kyuyamate, has become a street for the new generation. Hundreds of new families arrived with the construction of hundreds of apartment buildings on the side streets on the west side of Kyuyamate. I love this area. Once or twice a day, to

Gaston with a young girl on Children's Day, spring 1966.

balance the calm and the tranquillity of my *atelier*, I need to go out. I need to immerse myself in the crowds, *un bain de foule*, as we say in French, to mingle with people, life, noise, feel the tension and energy. I lose myself in the noise and the hubbub. It makes me appreciate the solitude of my studio more, the peace of my home. I confess, though, that sometimes I need to balance my Tokyo life. The tension of Tokyo becomes unbearable, and then I have to escape. A friend lends me his cottage at the seaside. In summer, the solitude of Champlain in Quebec bores me after a while. I miss the reviving pressure of Tokyo.

You have had a very full Tokyo life.

Yes, friendships with both Japanese and foreigners. There are hundreds of thousands of foreigners, white, and Asiatic. The Gerciks were a family that were very important to me. Abe was from Latvia, a Russian Jew from Riga, with no desire to ever go back. Lou was from Vancouver, not Jewish. She had gone to Kobe as a nurse before the war, and they met there.

How did you meet them?

Through a Jesuit artist, Joseph Love. The Gerciks were having a party for him to celebrate his ordination to priesthood, and he invited me along. They turned out to live only five minutes' walk from my studio, in a very nice Japanese-style house, but renovated with facilities—the western toilet, in other words—for foreigners. A week or two later, I was invited for dinner. They had several dinner parties a week. The invitations always came from Lou. She'd telephone: "Are you free?" And I'd simply say yes without bothering to check my schedule. If I had something else booked, I'd simply cross it off. I always knew it would be an enriching evening.

Everything was planned to the minute. 7:30 was arrival. Then there was one hour to meet the guests with a cocktail—this was the age of cocktails. At dinner, Abe was at one end, I was always on his right, and Lou was at the other end. The conversation was, as a friend put it, highly civilized. Abe and Lou were very open people, very cultured, very well read. They loved to meet people. They knew everything that was going on. I met astrologists, musicians, ambassadors, people from all walks of life, always interesting. At 10:30 we were up from the table, and at 11:00 we left. There were never more than eight. With more than eight, conversation is not possible. Everything was analyzed—I was young, I was learning.

Are the Gerciks still in Japan? I haven't heard you mention them.

No. They moved back to Canada. During the war—this is a dramatic story—they had gone to Vancouver. Lou was already in Canada, and Abe was supposed to cross. She heard on the news that his boat had sunk. It was the end for her. Ten days later, she received a phone call from Abe from Seattle. She said, "But the boat sank." He said, "Yes, but not the people on the boat."

When the war ended, they came back. I remain very close to the old couple—Abe is ninety-two now—and to Pat, the second child of three, and her family. The other two girls have forgotten their Japanese. Pat is very fluent, learned from the maids—a slight English accent. When I knew them, the girls were very young, students. Pat comes frequently. She is coming again in March. She works at MIT in Boston on an exchange programme of young researchers in Japanese companies and laboratories, so that the young scientists will know each other.

There is a very thoughtful inscription from James A. Michener in your copy of his *Japanese Prints: From the Early Masters to the Modern*. I know of

him as a novelist. I didn't realize that he had also done a book on Japanese prints.

He has had a strong interest in Japan. I'm not sure why. We met because of the art sale the Women's College Organization puts on every year—in October. You should go. It is an excellent way to add to your collection. The prints are exhibited by contemporary artists in Japan, and the profit goes to college scholarships for girls. I have almost all the catalogues since the first show forty years ago: you can see how sophisticated the shows have become, and how the quality of the work has improved.

The Yoseido Gallery was very, very helpful in gathering prints, but they had no space to collect the prints before the sale, or to spread out the works to make the selection for the show, so for the first years, I usually offered my space.

That fall, October 1971, James Michener was here. One of the women, a wife of a businessman or of one of the American Embassy people, knew him and asked him if he would like to participate in the judging. We had a good time making the selection of prints. A very pleasant afternoon. I already had his book, so I asked him to inscribe it.

People are always dropping by in Japan. It is one of the pleasures of living here.

Calligraphy: Abstract Art

One of the unique aspects of your work is your integration of Japanese forms, patterns, and

A calligraphy party at Itoh Sensei's home in Sendai in 1969. Both the father and daughter are teaching calligraphy.

sensibility. We talked about the way you incorporate the kimono; you have done the same with the *noren*, the half-curtain which is hung in doorways, and the ubiquitous Japanese shopping bags. You also work on traditional Japanese "canvas," i.e., the *byôbu*, the screen; or the *kakejiku*, the scroll. The manner in which you seem to abolish perspective with an overall distribution of forms and patterns —this is closer to an Eastern perception of art than Western.

In other words, you are saying that Japan has had a profound effect on me as an artist. Absolutely. First of all, training in calligraphy requires great concentration, steady control from the moment you dip the brush in the ink till you complete the *kanji* character or the text. There is no equivalent action in the West. In a way, the final product is present in the mind of the calligrapher at the time his brush touches the paper, but with calligraphy, no retouch is possible. The ink is on the paper. Forever. There must be no hesitation, even though the movement is executed rather slowly. So one must be absolutely sure of one's hand, of one's technique, and what one wants to write. That is one thing. My sensibility towards space owes much to calligraphy, too. Working on the floor makes you see differently than working on a wall. It is the opposite of dripping—Pollock—which is a free action. The gestural work I did in the sixties was influenced by the Sino-Japanese calligraphy I practiced, not by Pollock. In fact, I did not know Pollock's work at that time.

You say you studied calligraphy for two years.

With Hidai Nankoku. His method was very demanding. We began with the study of the old Chinese characters, up to the abstract contemporary forms, which developed both my discipline and the sense of the abstract. The roots of the abstract in my art, an understanding that a work is essentially based on form, are there, in Oriental calligraphy. The result was that almost all my work from my arrival in Japan until 1971 was "abstract." I was coming to terms with Delacroix, who said that a painting is only a surface on which shapes and colours are placed in a certain order. In this sense, all art is "abstract."

You see the result of my training in calligraphy in gestural paintings done in the sixties and the seventies in the four paintings *The Seasons* in the main lobby at the Canadian Embassy in Tokyo. I used *kanji* characters as the starting point, getting progressively more abstract through the first three seasons, *Spring*, *Summer* and *Fall*. *Winter* was entirely abstract. All of these paintings were done on the floor.

There are less obvious aspects of Japanese influence in my work. I make extensive use of colour gradation in paintings as well as in prints, a characteristic of the prints of the Ukiyo-e period. I used pebbles and stones in a baptismal font to evoke the Japanese stone garden. The lotus flower in a painting evokes the East; fruit, the West.

From what you are saying, it seems that calligraphy is as much art, drawing, as it is writing.

In fact, exactly the same instruments and materials are used in *sumi-e,* ink paintings, as in calligraphy. The same brushes, the same inks. So much so that in Japanese, writing and drawing is pronounced in the same way, and written with the same character: *kakou.*

If the Occident has tried since forever to clarify a mixture of letters, to refine the word to extract all its substance, the Orient has worked equally towards polishing the writing, the written line, and to give it an artistic aspect. In the Orient, the accent is put more on the calligraphy and the art of forming beautiful characters.

The Sino-Japanese characters are seductive even for the Occidental eye. There is a focus on proportion, form, and even colours. The way in which the characters are drawn/written can suggest greatness, nobility, and regularity. But, before all else, they must be true. The line that forms the character does not lie: it reveals the state of mind of the artist at the moment that this stroke is born in him. This stroke is life. In fact, we touch on a notion dear in the Orient and little known or ignored in our Western traditions: the line.

This idea of the stroke, the thought, the word, as life evokes the creation story of the Judeo-Christian-Muslim tradition, that in the beginning, as God "spoke" the word, life was created. They were simultaneous.

We see something similar in Hsieh Ho in his classification of painters in the fifth century. Calligraphy has deep roots in the past. Hsieh Ho had six basic principles of Chinese painting—which caused a great deal of ink to flow later on. The first and most important of these principles is the Ch'i. The *kanji* for Ch'i has four readings, four meanings: spirit, rhythm, life, and movement. For Hsieh Ho, the first meaning, spirit, took precedence. He is the only one who concerned himself with the exact definition of Ch'i in relation to calligraphy, actually. Hsieh Ho without a doubt believed in the development of the spiritual resources of the artist so he could express the Spirit, Tao's breath. In the context of Tao, this Spirit, this vital force, this vital rhythm, this "harmony of spirit which produces the movement of life" is fundamental. Ch'i expresses the harmony of nature, a harmony of Sky and Earth.

Spirit, life, rhythm, and movement: for me, these are complementary aspects found throughout Sino-Japanese painting and calligraphy: the beginning of

Gaston with assistant Isao Akagawa at the printing press, 1971.

my apprenticeship in art was in Japan in calligraphy and *sumi-e*.

I don't think that contemporary art, which strangely enough often resembles the Sino-Japanese calligraphic stroke, is able to claim the same spiritual source. We often see chaos, tearing, breaking-up, more than harmony and order.

The Print Studio: 18,726 Numbered and Signed

When did you turn to printmaking? How long after your study in calligraphy?

About five years after I arrived in Japan, so about three years after my study with Hidai Nankoku. Around 1965, another artist friend, Donald Robertson, decided to write a book on Japanese prints. He wanted to introduce the richness and the variety of Japanese printmaking to the Western world. He limited his choice of artists to a few printmakers who had original and specific techniques. One day he asked me to accompany him as a translator to interview Hiroyuki Tajima in Yokohama. It was like a lightning bolt. Hiroyuki Tajima was using a fairly simple technique, yet he produced spellbinding prints. I went to work as soon as I got back to my studio. For weeks, I experimented with techniques—particularly his.

Things happened very fast. At first I had an assistant, Isao Akagawa, who worked with me until 1977. When I started to print editions for other artists, the studio had to be modified and I trained some printers—as many as fifteen were working with us at one time. Between 1969 and 1972, we ran off an average of forty copies of forty different medium-sized editions per year. I was trying to achieve the finest gradation possible in lithography, and I often mixed several techniques in the same work. In 1975 the studio printed fifty-two editions. The studio became a large-scale operation. During the last six months of 1973, eighteen editions came off my presses. The catalogue I put together of my own prints in March 2001 lists 540 editions, a total of 18,726 prints printed by hand or with a craft press, and each of these prints was numbered and signed.

Many of the lithographers in Japan, some of the best studios, are artists who studied first with you.

Yes, but the tradition of lithography in Japan goes back to the nineteenth century. There were woodcuts, another way of printing, over a thousand years ago. We find prints of tiny Buddhas, in the second century. But lithography, which is printing on stone or a sheet of metal, was introduced in Japan by another priest, Father M.-M. Rotz; in 1868 in the month of August he printed a Christian calendar on a press which he had installed in the bishop's palace in Nagasaki. Later on, lithography was used commercially. A hundred years later, I bought a lithography press and quite a few stones in Osaka that still had the imprints for saki labels. When I started to work with Isao Akagawa, there were very few places in Japan where lithography was used artistically. Quite quickly, our studio started to become known throughout Japan. After all, the world of printmaking is not so big.

Why did you give up teaching?

When I started teaching in the mid-sixties, teaching had great importance for me. I was experimenting a lot at the time, and I was pushing my students in the same direction, both at Junshin College and in my own studio. I taught at Junshin for five years and out of my studio for about ten years, mostly printmaking to adults, both professionals and amateurs, although I have taught painting. I gave a lot, but I also got back a lot. The spirit was there and marvellous things happened. To my great joy, my former students are the ones who continue the tradition of the studio.

But the demands for conversion of chapels and churches were becoming more numerous, and the burning feeling for teaching and printing for others diminished. I was more and more conscious of not having the time to do my own work. So in 1977 I slowed the pace of production of prints for other artists and finally I stopped altogether. I reorganized my studio for my own personal use—it has been that way since 1980.

44 Modern Japanese Print Artists

You have written two books on printmaking, *44 Modern Japanese Print Artists*, and *Evolving Techniques in Japanese Woodblock Prints*, this one with another artist, Amadio Arboleda. Then you wrote another, *Children's Drawings*. What led you to take time from producing art to writing about art?

It was largely a result of the teaching and of producing prints. I had come to know the techniques of printmaking and the world of contemporary Japanese printmaking in the years 1960 to 1970 from A to Z. The vitality was extraordinary, and practically nothing had been written on the subject. I sensed a need, and my students and my friends strongly urged me to go ahead. I overlooked nothing in analyzing what was going on in printmaking in the 1960s and 1970s; I went through all the works in the Yoseido Gallery, the main gallery in Tokyo which specializes solely in prints; I interviewed dozens and dozens of printmakers all over Japan and even in New York, and while I was with them in their studios, I was able to analyze their work. It was also an excellent

Gaston and assistants at a litho press, 1975.

opportunity to assemble a collection, which I did. The book appeared simultaneously in English and Japanese.

A few years later, Amadio Arboleda, who was a student and became a close friend, suggested that we do a book on the techniques of woodblock prints in Japan, *Evolving Techniques in Japanese Woodblock Prints*. There was nothing like it in print at that time. Again, this book was written following interviews with the artists. It was a chance to familiarize myself with new techniques…and add to my collection of prints. The book sold out its print run rather quickly, I am proud to say. The subject matter is still current, but it has never been reprinted. I also wrote articles on the same subject for numerous journals around the world: Canada, France, Australia, Korea, Japan…

What led to the book, *Children's Drawings: From Early Scribblings to Human Figuration*?

Ah—a very small book about children and their scribblings, what kind of meaning they give to them.

Actually, I was teaching children as well. Or maybe it was more of a happening. On Saturday afternoon, the studio was open for Japanese children and foreign children, ages about four to twelve. I had huge tables set up. The ones that could scribble scribbled, and the ones who could paint painted. It was a couple of hours of fun with some direction, mostly for the older children, if they needed it. The younger children, I was observing. I went on, actually, to observe children in an international daycare centre in Tokyo as well as children in other countries.

Atelier Petit, 1976.

We think children are scribbling, but actually, it is research. All children follow the same pattern. At about one and a half years of age, they try to make a circle. All children do that. Eventually they manage to close the circle—monkeys and chimpanzees make a circle by chance once in a while. Once the child closes the circle, she/he starts to scribble inside until they see eyes. Then they start to "bar" the circle—some of the bars become hair, some stretch down and become legs, arms. At first, the arms come from the head, then they find the right position.

All children start the same way, and they all follow the same pattern. Some go on to develop themes, the theme of the princess, or of the house. What we adult artists call a series. I was especially interested in that because at that time I was myself working in series, *The Family Portrait* and *The Gesture of David.*

The Bag Priest of Shibuya

Your work is described by some as avant-garde. Would you agree with that?

Avant-garde…I don't know. I prefer to think that I am "of the present." I react to what is happening today, to the material world surrounding me today. If you had walked into one of my exhibitions a few years ago, you might have seen kimonos, three bed sheets, two pillows, one quilt, six window blinds, six *noren*, and hundreds of paper shopping bags, all objects devised for a specific purpose: to clothe, to cover people when they go to bed, to block light coming through windows, to partition space. All of these are material objects used by people in their daily lives.

I see these objects in a different way. I believe that the artist's function is to propose new worlds, personally and socially, worlds that are different from what people accept as "normal" and therefore valid: to *meta-morphose* things, objects, and life. One could say that art comes from an incredible attention to the imagination. We see the results as entirely new worlds. The world of Matisse, the world of Picasso, the world of Warhol, etc. What made Matisse flatten space as flat as a Persian carpet in *Harmony in Red* and in *The Red Studio*? And what made Picasso introduce Iberian and African forms when he painted *Les Demoiselles d'Avignon*? There were no rules to categorize or justify the specific selection of objects or the manner in which Matisse or Picasso painted them.

I pick up kimonos, bedsheets and pillow cases, a quilt, window blinds, *noren* and paper shopping bags and with those I initiate a new language, a new way to look at them. I give them a new function…with emotion. Imagination alone dictates.

I have heard you referred to as "the bag priest of Shibuya."

Ah. My recycled works. We live in a society which discards waste at an outrageous pace. We live in a society of *prêt à jeter*, if I may coin a phrase, ready to discard, to throw away. As early as the mid-sixties, the more aware I became of this tendency of contemporary society, the more resentful I became. In my way I started to recycle, and I've been recycling material for more than twenty-five years. But I have always been careful not to become exclusively a "recycling artist." I have always believed in balance in my activities in general and in art in particular. I avoid extremes.

What led you to the designing of church vestments?

The same thing that led me to church design. The last fifty years have seen huge changes. This was an exciting time in the church. Up to the second Vatican Council of 1964-65, there was no possibility of creativity, not in church design, not in vestments, not in the service, not, in fact, in any area.

This in spite of the creativity of old. Think of the Gothic churches. Incredible creativity. Think of the magnificent stoles worn by the officiating priests on the wall paintings of ancient churches of the Near Orient, for example, at Karyie Cami, in Istanbul.

I had been following the development of sacred art in Europe in magazines, *Sacred Art* and *Church Art* during my studies. The first chasuble I designed, I made no change to the garment. I designed only the cloth, which was woven by a weaver in Montreal. That chasuble was for a Dominican who was leaving for Africa. This was in 1960, just after I was ordained. A few years later in Japan, in 1963, I designed another chasuble which integrated an *obi,* the very wide belt—which can be very ornate—that women wear with the kimono. The one I used was a light cream and green colour.

My favourite of your chasubles is the one where the design on the back looks like stained glass.

That was about the same period, the mid-sixties. In 1965, when the Vatican Council recommended co-celebrations, I did another design in a simple light cloth. We wear different colours at different times of the year, red on bloody Sunday, for instance, so these were in different colours. Actually, I prefer an albe-chasuble of the monastic cowl type, in a pale colour, plain and simple, because on the whole we have to keep a certain decorum and a certain unity. The accent changed in the seventies to the stole, which is mostly the sign of priesthood.

Cloth is a plastic material for you, then, as much as when you incorporate the kimono or the *noren* into a painting.

You could say that. In some of my paintings, I have used printed cloth as the background. You see this in *The Stunning Message.* I used printed cloth again for the backdrop for the stage design I did for the opera in Korea. This spiral way of working—a change of material, in form, in colour—allows me great freedom, like a springboard that bounces me to other artistic experiences.

You made a mural of light cardboard in 1963 in the chapel in Kyoto, knowing it could not last. Why?

There was so much of this material in Japan. Paper. I wanted to use it. And at the time I did not know how long it would last. It lasted twenty-five years. It was an exploration. I replaced it in 1990 with a stained glass window, *La Dernière Cène, The Last Supper.* This will last much longer, I expect.

For me, though, this mural of cardboard paper was special. The students of the Catholic boys' school helped—they rolled 5,800 paper tubes in three colours, white, black and red, all the same length, ten centimetres, the diameters varying between three and seven centimetres. I placed the tubes in boxes with a glass surface, and the design was cut according to the coloured rolls. Each student who helped in the project wrote his name in the interior of a tube, and inserted it himself into the space of his choice. Ten and twenty years later, many of the students came to show their wives and children the spot where their names had been written.

A Lecture on Classicism

At the same time as you are described as "avant-garde," your work is also described as having "elements of classicism." Do you find a contradiction in this?

No. I believe in order or coherence in the structure of my work, in the feeling expressed through the intrinsic value of colour, line, form, regardless of the representational value. All in all, a general impression of orderliness, a certain simplicity, a balanced and controlled formal purity, puts my works in direct line with the classic and humanistic tradition of the West. Here I would add that, like classic European painting of the past, my paintings have content. In the past, Greek and Roman myths, religion, or humanistic values were the "subject" of art. You will find similar "signification" or "subject" in my art, although the expression is different. Because I am a priest, people usually expect me to produce work with obvious references to biblical scenes or events. There are plenty, but they are not obvious, as you know.

When I explain, of course, they understand. You, without the Christian symbolism in your background, respond to other aspects of my work, the juxtaposition of images from contrasting cultures and artistic periods, for instance. There is always more in a work than even the artist is aware of. We do not always know from where or what we create. It only proves my point, that a work lives through the viewer, and lives in a different way through each viewer. This is part of the magic of art, I would say.

The word "classic" came from Greece and ancient Rome when it was applied to literature. Culture at that time was based on man. And man was looking for the golden mean. From Aeschylus to Aristotle, excess was considered a sin as grave as thinking of oneself as equal to the gods. In this perspective, classicism appeared to be a triumph of reason and rational order, which gave man a significant and decisive role in the general harmony of the cosmos. Classicism evoked the qualities of order, equilibrium, harmony, simplicity, control.

This notion of classicism, a purely European notion, evolved under the Academy established in France in the time of Louis XIV. It became all-powerful, dictating to writers as well as to artists: all intimate personal feeling, capriciousness, and eccentricity had to yield to self-discipline, urbanity, correctness, and accepted standards of good form. The restrained style of Poussin was favoured over the passionate exuberance of Rubens, because Poussin's pictorialism could more readily and demonstrably be reduced to a system of formal values based on geometrical principles. Rubens's style was so personal, impetuous, voluptuous, and violently emotional that it always remained a bit beyond the grasp. In academicism nothing eccentric, nothing unpredictable was allowed to creep in and destroy the general impression of orderliness. The pictorial standards were based on formal purity, demonstrable mathematical relationship, logical definition, and rational analysis. These were the qualities which came to designate classicism, a term which indicated the highest standard based on a tradition of excellence.

Although the measuring sticks of symmetry, order, regularity, dignity, reserve and clarity put forward by the Academy degenerated to downright regimentation and conventionalism, nevertheless, the true creative spirit pushed in new directions. In the case of artistic geniuses, it has always been accompanied by a certain break-up, as for instance when Giotto was breaking away from the pathetic Byzantine tradition; when Leonardo da Vinci, this encyclopaedic mind, was marking the passage between the art of the quattrocento to that of the Renaissance; when Matisse was flattening space to introduce decoration; and when Picasso was exploding the accepted rules of painting learned from Cézanne, introducing new influences and opening the way to abstract art, without ever falling into it.

In the first decades of our century, painters and sculptors broke with the long-established tradition of their art as an art of representation. The artist came to believe, to quote Meyer Schapiro, that what was essential in art, given the diversity of themes or motifs, were two universal requirements: that every work of art have an individual order or coherence, a quality of unity and necessity in its structure regardless of the forms used; and, second, that the forms and colours chosen have a decided expressive physiognomy, that they speak to us as a feeling-charged whole, through the intrinsic power of colour and line, rather than through the imaging of facial expressions, gestures, and bodily movements, although these are not necessarily excluded—for they too are forms. …I have just given you another lecture. And I suppose you will insist that others besides yourself will actually be interested.

I can certainly say that you've explained "classicism" more clearly and succinctly than I remember when I was doing art history. But I'll put it in a heading so that people who aren't interested can skip it.

What is "beauty," if I may ask? Do you strive to achieve "beauty"?

Good question. I am happy to provide you with an answer. Notice, I do not say "the" answer. I leave room for another interpretation or approach.

St. Thomas Aquinas defines beauty as "the splendour of the true." Thomas Mann in *Death in Venice* says beauty "is the only form of the immaterial that we can perceive by our senses and which our senses can bear." In my work I have always tried to present pieces which are true, which give pleasure to the senses, and which raise the spirit, by which I mean I try to emphasize "presence" and density, qualities which leave a mark on the spirit of those who see them.

I'd venture to say that there is beauty in my work, a beauty which is the result of the balance of colour, form, material, and the inherent composition of the work. But there are many more nuances to consider in defining beauty. Suffice it to say that I have never rejected the aesthetic aspect which I think should be part of every work of art. It is recognized that the specific, the keenly somatic and authentically felt, is a must in every real work of art, and I consider that these same qualities can be found in my work. Or, at least, it is what I am looking for.

Picasso: A Painter with a Chisel in His Hand

Are you conscious of influence by the works of other artists?

Many artists and for many different reasons. The question is complex. I remember having studied Giotto quite thoroughly, for instance. With Giotto, perspective, emotion, and individualism were born; dramatic realism in art emerged from the grip of Byzantium severity. In the basilica of Assisi where he painted his frescoes of the life of St. Francis, we see the beginnings of the Renaissance and of self-knowledge. Giotto's natural, emotional rendering of religious themes and Fra Angelico's work both mesmerized me. I lectured on them in the early sixties. I also fell in love with the strength of Michelangelo's paintings, his lively figures, his use of pure colours. What can one say about the expressive force of a Michelangelo? Then came Chardin with his sense of mystical light, the turbulent Turner—

Closer to our time, there was van Gogh; the group *Les Fauves*, Gauguin, in particular; followed by Rouault, then Matisse and Picasso. I'm at odds with Picasso. I don't think much of him as a painter.

Yet he is considered a genius, credited with revolutionizing painting in this century.

Yes, undoubtedly, Picasso was a genius. He is an unbeatable master of the line, yet, to me, his mind is more that of a sculptor even when he uses paint. A sculptor with a brush in his hands, or a painter with a chisel in his hands. He knows how to analyze an object, split it apart, and give it back to us in his own way. He pushed forward, to the point of explosion, the main techniques offered to the artist of his time: sculptures, prints, collages. He also knew when a theme had come to an end: his *Blue* and *Rose* series, his thorough analysis of cubism. Matisse was a master of the line and maybe the last painter of the century. In his work, drawing becomes life. Then there was Alexei von Jawlensky, the peace and withdrawal in his series of figures. His work was the inspiration for my series *Utopique conservatoire de l'humanité*. Paul Klee, Louise Nevelson, Antoni Tàpies, Pierre Soulages, Francis Bacon, Giorgio de Chirico—all of them have attracted me at one time or another.

Today's art I consider much too verbal. If you can present your production in a beautifully balanced series of words, more often obtuse than refined, you are said to be a good artist. But art is first "visual," something that is made to be seen, and not so much talked about. What is purposely provocative or shocking makes the news: a sculpture made of fresh meat, carcasses of sheep in formaldehyde, etc., but a constant development of a subject like the recent extraordinary drawings of antique works of art by Jim Dine rarely does.

Young people tend to think their role should be, as they say, "to point out the hypocrisies and weaknesses of our society." A critic like Grombrich would say that of course our society has its vices and its weaknesses, plenty of them, but civilization is a great achievement of mankind. We don't want to go back to barbarism. It is easier to destroy this very tenuous achievement, this very thin layer of civilization which mankind has achieved, than to replace it.

Installations and Michelangelo

What do you think of some of the newer movements in art? Installations, for instance.

Installations—to pile up seven logs against a wall, place a bucket with yellow water in front of them, cover the floor with freshly cut hair picked up at the nearby barber shop and hang a single red bulb in the centre of the room, or to spread hundreds upon hundreds of foil-wrapped candies on a floor in a rectangular shimmering silver carpet measuring two by four metres and weighing 2,000 pounds... Can I call these installations art?

The first description is mine, invented on the spot for your benefit, and I have no doubt it would do well in "modern" museums. And probably make me a lot of money, too. The second installation with the foil-wrapped candies was displayed at the Guggenheim Museum in New York and in Chicago, and the dimensions, it seems, can vary. It was said that "the piece refers to the AIDS epidemic and the lack of a cure or even care that so many suffering from the disease must face." Do you see the reference? I don't.

Such "artists" and those who write about them have to substantiate the display with words that, for me, have no relation to what one sees. Is it Art? It all depends how one defines art. Art has many faces. This is a face I do not recognize. For me, it isn't the creative imagination that triggers their art, but a program they want to achieve. A social or political program. *My Home Sweet Home in Ruins: Urban Environment and Art in Japan*, on view at the Setagaya Museum a few summers ago, centred on themes such as inflated land prices, loss of traditional culture, and destruction of the environment. To these themes we may add: artists of colour, women artists, AIDS, and so on. I must say that much of this activity is quite alien to me. I simply don't see the point of much of it. For me, these displays are hardly worth the effort. They leave me cold. It's certainly why I visit galleries and contemporary art museums less and less.

In the past, artists were busy trying to survive, having to please patrons, following guilds, or were involved in producing religious art. The freedom for artists to be so outspoken is relatively new.

Yes, it is a new phenomenon in art.

Okay—tell me about a show you would make a great effort to see.

Ah—if we want to talk about works which have positively affected me—let me tell you about one of the greatest works in artistic history. The Sistine Chapel. The first time I visited was before the cleaning, so the frescoes were smeared with black smoke. My dream was to return to see it in all its original vividness. The opportunity came up during the meeting and exhibition of Dominican artists in Rome in November 2000. Getting to the chapel was a story in itself. Possibly because I did it in a way that I do not always do things, I followed orders, and how one approached the chapel was now "ordered."

The day before I was to leave Rome I left the group to go by myself to the Sistine—how the others—all artists—were able to pass this up, I have no idea. There was—no surprise—a long line at the entrance. Once I got inside, I headed in the direction of the Sistine Chapel, and I faithfully followed the arrows. Arrow after arrow, I climbed stairs, went through room after room strung together like the beads of a rosary, down corridors whose ends disappeared into a vanishing point, and yet more stairs, going up or going down. With

Gaston in his Tokyo atelier. Paintings and aluminium sculptures, 1985.

every kilometre I became more incensed. The museum was overflowing with superb works, but it wasn't those I wanted to see, it was the chapel.

I still resent whoever it is who planned this absurd, meandering course forcing you to traipse through all those endless corridors, going up and down all those stairs before tasting the beauty of the Sistine Chapel. One could say "the fruit for which one waits tastes even sweeter." I'm not sure. I would have had more time to savour this unique work if I had gone directly to the chapel. I have bitter memories of the time lost going through those endless corridors…and I pity the elderly with leg problems!

When I finally reached it, I was not in good humour. I was footsore, exhausted and short-tempered—but what splendour! The cleaning definitely revealed what Michelangelo had wanted, these finely wrought figures, these rich, lush colours. I fell into an enchanted stupor. In my series *The Gesture of David*, there are extremely muscular characters, which is quite unusual. No doubt *The Last Judgement* was affecting my subconscious at that time.

Cufflinks and Styrofoam

Your work is in all sizes, from cufflinks, to prints, to—well, the design of an entire church.

Size has nothing to do with art, but size is not a factor that can be ignored. More than the image itself, when I am about to start a work I usually visualize the product in a very definite size. When I decide to make myself a pair of cufflinks out of a Chinese jade bracelet, I have to keep in mind that these cufflinks have a job to do at the end of my sleeves, so they can hardly exceed a certain volume and weight. When I decide to do a painting, I first select a canvas or a surface of a given size and proportion. The same when I make a stained glass window, since it has to fit in a specific space. When I do a mural, like that at the Matsuda Fire Station or the exterior wall of the Franciscan-Conventual Seminary in Sekimachi, size is one of the first factors. The second factor is the material—concrete, aluminium, glass, bronze? And this, of course, depends on factors such as location, budget and the wishes of the patron. The artist is also inspired by constraints, the imaginations, the ideas, the desires of the other. Incorporating the needs and the imagination of the other is part of the challenge.

I like working on small projects: I constantly make drawings on *shikishi*, small cardboards with gold borders, fourteen by twelve centimetres in diameter. But large spaces are a challenge that I enjoy taking up. Maybe my preference is to work on large surfaces. Give me a wall, and I will make it live. On this point I may be Aristotelian: was it not he who said "nature abhors a vacuum"? Two or three times, I have done stained glass windows which spread over 100 square metres. My largest mural is made of bronze, which I just finished for the Church in Nagasaki in the autumn of 2000. It measured three-and-a-half metres by seven-and-a-half metres, and its finished weight was 3,500 kilos. Maybe it is because my youth was spent in a vast country, the horizon was boundless…

You say you don't have a preference for size. Do you have a preference for material?

I can work with any material: pencil, colour, oil, clay, styrofoam, glass, etc. In a way, the material has no importance. But at the same time I have to say that the material is very important, because it makes me study all the possibilities and, after, to work within its confines, its nature. So I work differently when I use paper, canvas, glass… I am very aware of the material that I use. I have the greatest respect for it. I want to give it the maximum expression while recognizing and submitting myself to its limitations. And, too, the material can be given new meaning.

Given meaning in the sense in which you give new meaning to the *noren* and the kimono?

Yes. This is an interesting point. I've just read an article by Michael Lonsdale in the March 2001 issue of *Actualities of Religions* which addresses this point, this idea of paying attention to the materials of the artist. Matter, the material, is part of creation, so why would the matter itself not pray to the creator? Lonsdale says, and I quote, "The matter does not express itself, but it is there. It is given, in an elementary fashion, in tubes of paint, and the artist's hand works it and transcends it…Today, many artists throw the matter, almost spit the paint on the canvas. The matter/material is not considered. There is no love. When you look at a panel of Klee, of Turner or of Titian, you can see all the good will they have towards the matter, they caress the oil. The colours of Bonnard, of Matisse, are they not signs of happiness? I do not paint to make progress. I paint because I have to. God lives in the creation. That is true in every act of sincere art."

A Newly Coated Canvas

What do you think of art by computer?

It is no doubt a question of sensibility, but I do not think it is for me.

Have you tried?

George Baier of Montreal is an art professor who is among the best in his field. We sat together an entire day exploring all the possibilities. It was incredible. On the screen in front of me were all the effects, all the textures of all the materials an artist could desire. Fascinating. Totally arresting…

But?

But I am old-fashioned. I start first by choosing a surface, a format of a certain size, say, a two-by-two-metre surface. Then, as an example, say that I apply a square of red liquid pigment seventy by seventy centimetres in size. The paint runs a little. My eye, my sensitivity, a certain visual shock aroused by the red shape will lead me to apply the following shape of a certain colour and a certain size. In the present case, the red dominates. It is my sensitivity confronted by what I see which dictates the following stages, so that all is balanced. A different artist would react in a different way.

When I work on the computer, the size of the screen constricts me. Suppose I did not paint on the large two-by-two metre surface. But I have the same composition in my head. Necessarily, the red square will be a lot smaller: it will be in proportion to the size of the screen. Will the same picture result? I don't think so. Looking at this small square, my eye will not react in the same way as when I use the large format. The next choice of shape will no doubt be different because the impact on the eye is different. You might argue that I could enlarge the impression I see on the screen. I could expand this to a canvas two-by-two metres in size. I can give it texture. The result? An enlarged composition, a print done in a mechanical fashion. It comes out of the keyboard and the mouse! And because the psychological and physical process is completely different, the product is something else.

I react strongly to the space where I work, to the smell of a newly coated canvas, to the smell of the paint, the turpentine. I have to work with my hands, get them dirty if necessary, I have to touch, I have to move. For me, it is very important to struggle with what I do. It is not so much the effect of mastering the matter as of communicating what I feel with love. "To tame it," would say the Little Prince.

Do you feel that a work done on the computer is a work of art?

That is for others to say. But I recognize that for graphics, the computer is an excellent instrument.

A work of art, whether it is an icon, a sculpture, a painting or a simple drawing, is an object, nothing more. As I've said before, the work comes to life only as a result of the attention we give it, which is different according to the experience/sensibility, artistic or historic, of each individual. What will the reaction be to the same work tomorrow, next year, a century from now? The answer will always be different. We can't know the answer, and I think this element is sufficiently captivating that an artist finds himself pushed by the attraction of recognition. My goal as an artist is to go beyond, to bring the spectator to an astonishment. Which is, I think, the aim of art. But this wonder finds itself in the eye of the beholder.

I want to pick up on something you just said—that when you work, you have to get your hands dirty, to touch, to move. Yet once a work is finished, we are never allowed to touch. You have said that you like to use all the five senses when you appreciate—or study—a work.

It is understandable that in a gallery or museum one is forbidden to touch the works. It is most of all for reasons of security or preservation. But to really "get the feel" of a work, we have to touch it, manipulate it. It all depends on the dimensions, of course, but I have to take a panel, a print or a sculpture in my hands. I have to touch the work, to look behind, in front, I must smell it, weigh it. We appreciate a work of art with the eyes, the hands, the nose and the heart. It is a very physical experience, sensual and emotional. It is a bit like a book.

The Noh Mask and the Bellelli Family

You have done at least nine series. The first three series, *Creation*, *Bulles*, and *Bleue*, are abstract. You were painting figuratively, though, when you arrived in Japan. Your first show as chaplain on Vancouver Island was all figurative work. The study of calligraphy led to a complete shift to the abstract.

Yes, it did. Absolutely. Although you probably wouldn't see a clear direct influence, except in a paintings like *The Seasons.* My first series, *Creation*, was very cosmic. There was a black background, lacquer poured directly onto large wooden panels, or mixed lacquer and cement powder to create a texture, or there was added Nihonga coloured powder. I used a sprayer, as well, so there was a very cosmic effect. It was this first series, dozens of paintings, that led to my first exhibition in Tokyo in 1963.

The series that followed, *Bulles*, was floating forms, luminous, and moist, done with transparent colours, which conjure up a fantasy world. I made ten large canvases, all painted on the same day, January 15, 1967. The series *Bleue*, begun in 1968, was also an exploration of the cosmic. In this series, I first painted large shapes on the canvas with acrylic pigments, then I covered the entire canvas with a solution of cobalt blue paint diluted in turpentine and varnish. Finally, I used the spray gun again, applying black shapes and creating a mystical atmosphere. Maybe this exploration of the inner dried me up. I don't know. But I do know that it was impossible for me to go any further in non-representation. I put away my brushes—and the spray gun—for two long years. Well, honestly, I can say that the spray gun had very little use after that.

How did you feel about this artist's block? Did you panic?

No, because I was doing so many other things. I was doing prints, I was working on some aspect of design in a number of different churches. It was only the painting that was stuck. That was at the end of 1968. If you look at the prints of that period, 1969-70-71, I did forty editions a year.

In any event, with no special help from me, the darkness dissipated, the sun came out, with a small series. I never gave this series a name, but perhaps we could call it *Checker Board*. Each canvas was latticed; each incorporated pieces of stained glass. The light dazzles. The thick paint and the light colours of these small canvases are no doubt a reaction to the mysterious darks of the previous series.

You returned to the figurative with your series *Eyes*.

Yes, in 1971, February 7th. Yes. I started with the eyes. Shapes, human heads with eyes, millions of eyes that come out of nothingness. Very few of these canvases from the *Eyes* series have been shown to the public, but I always liked their spontaneity, their strength. I actually consider these canvases as a follow-up to the thirty or so painted works on canvas or on paper that I did in Paris during the winter 1964-1965, which focuses on disembodied heads and the eyes.

Following the series *Eyes*, I let myself be won over by the human form, and I added the body. The trigger this time was Degas's *The Bellelli Family*. I was deeply attracted to this painting, the geometric forms, the triangles in particular. I reflected a long time on it to gain the strength, and then I spent two long years on the series, *The Family Portrait*. The result was over 580 works: drawings, paintings, prints and sculptures.

In *The Family Portrait*, we see the forms split apart, two hands, two feet, a head. This series was done between 1971 and 1973. Why is that?

I'm not sure. Maybe it was a premonition. By the eighties, it was clear that the family structure was indeed splitting apart, to the extent that 1994 was declared The Year of the Family. I didn't have a conscious sense of the family in crisis, but if there was something of premonition in my work, then there is definitely hope for the family, because in my series, there is a kind of resolution. Finally, near the end of the series, the rounded, smooth forms have a kind of calm to them.

You have mentioned spiralling back in your work. Is *Family Portrait* a series that you still come back to?

I took up the theme again a few years later, but after about twenty drawings and eight canvases, it was finished. It is impossible to go further. Now I sense that the vein is definitely exhausted.

In your next series—this is in 1973, after *Family Portrait*—you began the series, *Geste de David, The Gesture of David*. Aside from the obvious, the events around David in the Bible, David with the harp, the anointing of David, David and his knights, David constructing an altar for God—Michelangelo's work was a trigger.

Yes, but unconsciously. I only realized that during my second visit to the Sistine Chapel in 2000. The muscularity of David, the gesture of David reaching his hand toward Bathsheba in her bath.

Stylistically, I started where I had left off with *Family Portrait*, that is to say, with rounded, geometric forms. The evolution was very fast at first, but after approximately twenty canvases, I had reached a wall. I stopped painting for a period of six months. The following year, though, I had a renewed vision of the subject. This second phase resulted in about sixty canvases, and a few prints. Very few drawings.

You were clearly doing figurative work again in the series *La monde à sa rupture, The World at its Rupture.*

That was in 1976, just after *La Geste de David* series. The basic idea is what I call cultural collages, or cultural citations. I borrow elements of existing works which I paste in a fantasy fashion—which brings me closer, and in spite of myself, to surrealism.

In fact, you see a bit of this borrowing in the *David* series, which is not yet figurative. In *Bathsheba in Her Bath*, a small Noh mask is tucked in the bottom corner. There is another Japanese reference—David is always purple; purple is a noble colour in Japan.

Why the Noh mask? What is the reference?

The Noh mask represents the self. People don't see themselves—the "self." They may know themselves, but they don't see themselves. In *Bathsheba in Her Bath*, King David hides. He goes against normal conscience. He wants another man's wife. He puts his hand towards the woman in her bath. He hides from himself—the Noh mask reminds him.

This method of using cultural citations really began then—and continues.

Why "cultural citations"?

To insert one or more sections of an existing work in another work is like using a citation in writing. I use iconographic fragments belonging to different western or oriental cultures to give them a new meaning. I talked earlier about the citation from Picasso's *Les Demoiselles d'Avignon.* I use photographs sometimes, too. Each fragment used is an "object" with its own identity and its own value. I extract this "object" from its context and place it in a contemporary context, mine. The whole produces a new reality, which reaches the level of the symbol—a symbolic realism, not a surreal realism, even though—yes—certain parts of the picture and certain technical effects of surrealism are sometimes used quite freely.

This process is different from that of the surrealist, whose goal is to utilize all the psychic forces—dreams, the unconscious.

To tell the truth, this is one series I do not think will ever be finished or closed, although in January 1986 there was an intermission. One day, I found myself in an acrobatic mood, and start playing with the elementary forms of the square, the triangle, and the circle—maybe a subconscious return to the forms drawn on my mother's ironing board. These elementary forms transformed into bottles, hundreds of fantastic bottles. Within seven weeks, I had done thirty-four canvases in oils, and in many of these canvases, I added collages of Japanese paper. They are all on the square, some of them quite small, forty-five centimetres by forty-five centimetres; some medium size, ninety centimetres by ninety centimetres; and some quite large, 1.8 metres by 1.8 metres.

Memory's Pleats (IV, VI, XII), 1988.

The series you are working on now, *Man's Memory*, has a very grand scope. It has a sense of culmination.

Maybe I am in search of liberation. In the words of one of your people, Baal Chem Tov, the founder of the Hassidic movement, "memory is the source of liberation and forgetfulness is the source of exile."

It could be also that when we reach a certain age, memory is very precious. *Man's Memory* is not composed so much of thought as of emotional pulsations.

But yes, perhaps *Man's Memory* is a culmination. For one thing, it encompasses four other series: *Memory's Wells* are paintings done on *shikishi,* cardboard—this is a tradition in Japanese painting; *Memory's Pleats* are done on *oridehon*, the folding books: *Memory's Jump Start* is done on roll-down window blinds; *Memory's Wanderings* is a series of prints. If you look at these works in one way, you can see a resemblance to a quilt. Or you can find profiles resembling particular aspects of pre-Columbian art. Columbian art has had a deep impression on me, as you know. It is the one collection I have not yet "used up." One thing is consistent, though. I finally realized that all of these works have a tie-in: the forms are "cut," the same as we cut stained glass. I work this way in both stained glass and paint, although sometimes I add interest to the surface of the canvas with paper collages or cloth.

Which brings me back to the influence of the comic strips when I was very young and I was tracing shapes and filling in colour.

This series picks up a whole lot of my past. So, yes, in that sense, a culmination.

Gaston working on a stained glass design, 1998.

Fully Clothed Lovers

One of your "cultural citations" is the nude, the *Odalisque* by Ingre. The nude is very much a part of the western tradition of art, is it not? In the erotic art of Japan, the *ukiye-o*, woodcuts of the Floating World, the geishas and the tea houses of the Edo period—a red-light district for the upper classes, essentially—the lovers, even in the act of congress, are clothed in elaborate kimonos. The only "nudes" I recall is a print of women at the bath, old women, young women, children, a fight going on—and there is no focus on the body. Rather than the body being defined, the form is suggested, more in the tradition of Matisse.

There you hit on an interesting point. Indeed, the nude has been an essential theme in Western art since the Greeks invented it in the fifth century before Christ. The study of the nude has been essential in Western art for the last several centuries.

One of the few classes I ever took in art was a course on the nude at a gallery in Shibuya, which became a classroom at night. Once a week, there were live models, although rather than an entire nude figure, I seemed to like to focus on a single feature with a very fine point. Some of these drawings were made into prints.

There is an excellent analysis of the history of the nude in a book by Kenneth Clark, *The Nude*, and we see artists swing between the male nude and the female nude. In Michelangelo's period in Florence, from 1480 to about 1505, a battle amongst nude males was considered the highest artistic subject, perfect physical beauty. The pendulum didn't swing back until the end of the nineteenth century. From that point on, the male nude as a subject is rare.

What about Rodin with his massive, muscular male nude sculptures?

You are thinking of *The Thinker* and *Three Shadows*. There is also Brancusi's *The Torso* ...these sculptures are all asexual. Matisse, as well, with few exceptions, paints only the female nude.

The female body attracts artists for diverse reasons. There is the sensual, sexual, erotic aspect in a nude study, but there is something else that may even be unconscious. The female nude attracts because of the shapes, which are fuller, more rounded than those of the male. She is often plump, chubby. Look at her hips, her breasts, and her thighs. A trifle, you will say, but a very important trifle. Whereas with a male nude, it is the muscles which attract. To each his own beauty.

Did you see the exhibition of Picasso's erotic art in Montreal in the summer of 2001?

Yes, and what a contrast to his works in the 1950s. He did a series of ten drawings in the winter of 1953-1954, an ironic commentary on the painter-model relationship, a commentary on nude painting as an element of the academic system. The model takes the advantage and the painter cuts a sorry figure: the young woman is a satisfied animal, a work of nature, more gracious and more alive than the painter will ever be able to realize on his canvas.

Then we see Picasso's erotic exhibition which, by the way, was also held in Paris and Barcelona. This was a series he inaugurated on February 18, 1970, a diffused cycle of disquieting strange behaviour where the women are constantly touching themselves. The men are ghost men in high hats. The men are continually looking, but not touching themselves, or anyone else. In fact, in this exhibition, Picasso presents himself as a sexual pervert.

If we look at these paintings, the women are all curved, round, in circles, whereas the men stand as vertical lines, rigid, wearing angled collars. Picasso, unlike the ancient painters, is not interested in muscles. Both Matisse and Picasso take delight in the curved forms, which, as we know, are symbols of perfection.

Aren't you going to ask about the Canadian influence in my work?

Absolutely—later.

The Self-Portrait

You've done a number of self-portraits, the first in 1959 where you are wearing your Dominican robe—very fitting as a symbol of, by then, the seven years of silence you had completed in that robe.

Yes. I am in a long tradition: Velázquez, Rembrandt, Goya, Albert Dürer, Leonardo de Vinci, Ingres, Dégas, and Cézanne, Manet, Monet, Ensor, Gauguin, Modigliani, Van Gogh—Van Gogh did twenty-eight, all in the last two years of his life, between 1886 and 1888. Then we can add Dali, Giacometti, Matisse, Picasso. Even artists who have never or almost never painted a face, landscape specialists like Pissaro, Utrillo, Palencia; abstract painters like Tapies or Miro; sculptors like Rodin and Moore—each and every one of them one day installed themselves in front of a mirror and set to work.

Some say that one of the major reasons an artist turns to self-portrait is that it is cheap. No need to hire a model. Certainly, Van Gogh didn't have a lot of money for models.

Even if you can afford them, models get tired. It's hard to keep a single pose without moving. The self-portrait allows the freedom of all possible variations without having to worry about the model, without leaving your quarters, and without costing a cent. A bargain.

What about the charge that self-portraits are merely narcissism?

That is too simple. Let me put forward the argument of one art critic—this was in the foreword to

Gaston with self-portraits, February 1988.

the catalogue of *The Art of Portraits in the XIX and XX Centuries in France.* It states the case well: "When the artist paints his likeness, he does not like it, he paints it."

I've done eight self-portraits, the first in 1959, then others in 1964, 1973, 1974, 1977-78, 1982, 1987, and 1988. I don't know if I will do another.

I would add another dimension, that when the artist paints his own portrait, he is fixing his likeness in time as an object, before his disappearance, or his disintegration. We might look at the self-portrait as a denial of death. In that sense, the portrait and the self-portrait have a truth similar to the landscape or the still life. Which is no doubt why there have been so many portraits commissioned since the very first one in the European tradition, which was King Jean le Bon, around 1350. It is a bid for immortality. For the artist, this has been a very good thing—many an artist has been sustained through the centuries on commissions for portraits.

Have you done commissioned portraits?

Not really. I've done portraits, but, if you see the list, you understand that it has not been with the intention of making my fortune—my Franciscan Uncle Barthélemy in 1955, my Grandmother Héroux in 1960, my sister Jacqueline, my brother, my brother-in-law, three or four of my friends.

At one point, I intended to do a series of portraits with prints in parallel, which I would call simply *Portraits.* I don't know quite how or why, but the project barely got started. What was left of this grand intention was ten canvases titled *Faces of My Mother,* all done in 1975. In 1976, I combined portrait and self-portrait, *The Painter and His Model*, me with my mother. I am in complete accord with Matisse when he says, "The study of portraits is a source of interest without end," but I went on to something else.

You asked me earlier why I never painted my father. I've thought about it, but I still have no answer. There is something mysterious about the choice of subject.

Since the 1960s, you have collaborated with about a dozen architects on more than fifty Roman Catholic churches and chapels in Japan, and this includes interior design, stained glass windows, religious furniture such as tabernacles, altars, candlesticks, baptismal fonts, murals... How were these collaborations realized?

Either I make specific pieces myself—a crucifix, a series of Stations of the Cross—or I prepare the design, which is carried out by assistants or specialists, here or abroad. For the stained glass windows, I do full-size drawings, indicating all the colours. For an object like an altar or a tabernacle, I might give both specific dimensions and general aspect. It really depends on the situation.

Let's take one project, your most recent, your collaboration with the architect Hideyo Oka on the Shiroyama Church in Nagasaki.

Oka-san contacted me early in 1999. I've worked with him on about a dozen projects. He's Catholic, actually, so this might explain his interest and his knowledge of churches. His firm—he's the director of the ICD architectural firm—had just gotten the contract to rebuild a church on the site of the original church. The entire front section of the church, the sanctuary, would be left up to me. He also wanted to have stained glass windows at the front of the church, which faces north, a good idea, since the sun doesn't come in through that angle, so it would give interesting light.

Some time later, he told me that a local bronze foundry was eager to do something—an example of how the desires and wishes of others can inspire. Mr. Nishida, the owner of the foundry, is also Catholic, so he had heard about the rebuilding of the church.

I came up with the idea of installing a bronze mural behind the altar, which would hide the entrance to the sacristy, and using bronze for the entrance doors at the front of the church to create a balance. And why not add a bronze panel of *The Last Supper* in front of the altar? There was time to think about it—construction was scheduled only for the year 2000. The bronze panel proved to be an enormous project. The styrofoam forms that you were walking around, thirty-two of them, were for the standing wall behind the altar. When it was finished, the mural weighed about 3,500 kilos.

In the fall of 1999, I received the final blueprints of the structure, and only then did I begin to plan more precisely. Up till then it had been simply ruminating. At the end of November, I had to go to Nagasaki to present my ideas to the pastor and a group of parishioners representing the parish. I also wanted to visit the foundry, to see the kind of work they produced. I needed to know if they could fulfill my expectations.

Can you describe that day? It wasn't very long after you had recuperated from an operation, I remember.

It was a day typical of my life, I would say. I left home at 7:00 a.m. for Haneda Airport to join Mr. Oka and Mr. Nagasu, the architect responsible for the construction. The airplane was delayed, so we didn't arrive in Nagasaki until 11:00 a.m. Mr. Nishida, the manager of the bronze factory, was waiting for us, and we headed straight to the foundry on the opposite side of the city. We discussed the various materials that could be used to make the forms, clay, styrofoam, etc., the different compositions of bronze, the percentage of copper, zinc, and so on, according to the effect or the colour

Altar with bronze mural of The Last Supper in Shiroyama Church, Nagasaki, 2000.

we wanted to have. In short, it was a technical discussion. Mr. Nishida was most eager to explain everything in detail in order to convince me that he could cast the forms in whatever material I selected. And I admit that he convinced me. From what I had seen in the factory, and from his experience...

On to lunch. As you know, Nagasaki has not only a long Christian tradition, but a longer tradition of good fish. So after a delicious meal of sushi, we headed for the old Shiroyama Church—a lovely site. The church and the school are surrounded by an old grove of trees—I know, you're going to ask me what kind of trees. Green trees. Tall trees. Probably cedar. It was November, and they still had their leaves.

We arrived there just in time for the 2:00 p.m. meeting. Sixteen people, including the pastor, an American priest of the Augustine Order, were expecting us.

I showed sketches of the mural. Well, "sketch" is too precise a word. I sketched as I spoke. I told them that I was thinking of many panels, of different sizes and forms, held away from the concrete wall by metal bars of different lengths, the whole making a sort of mosaic of bronze panels. The texture would be worked out as the work progressed.

The general idea was to insert, either engraved or in relief, very short excerpts from the Bible in different languages: Hebrew, Greek, Latin, Spanish, Japanese, Portuguese, Dutch. I wanted to underline the languages in which the Bible had entered Japan—through Nagasaki, in fact, so it was most fitting. Nagasaki was the port where the Jesuits from Portugal landed in the seventeenth century. Francis Xavier, actually.

I had been thinking of glass and bronze for the panels. Similar shapes in bronze would sandwich the glass, leaving sections of the glass untouched. Difficult to visualize, but I had brought an album with an example of a door I had done in the past. I hadn't yet decided on the motif or the design of the bronze for the doors. The stained glass windows would be in a style which I have developed over the years—more photos. The parishioners had questions, but they concerned the architect more than me. One point they insisted on, though, and this *was* my problem: they wanted to keep the sculpture of Christ on the cross hanging in the old church. It meant that I would have to incorporate it into the mural.

But a solution came to me in the plane on the way back that evening. I thought of a way to insert it into the mural so it wouldn't be too noticeable. I was home, problem solved, by 9:00 p.m.

What was the problem?

The sculpture is a little large, and made of plaster unfortunately, lightly painted, although the form is quite acceptable. It depicts Christ resurrected, hands upward, and clothed in a long gown.

Baptismal font in Shiroyama Church, Nagasaki, 2000.

Did you ever have any interest in actually doing the architectural planning?

No, and I have never had any intention of learning architecture, either. The technical knowledge of architecture would hamper me. This way, I am free in the way I perceive spaces, give orientations, create forms. If I had to consider the technical aspect, I might be more conservative. I preferred influencing the architects, not replacing them. In other words, working with the denominators. They are from Japan, anyway. They have influence that I don't.

The Gold Chalice and the Emerald Buddha

Both Buddha and Jesus were against materialism. How do you think they would feel, confronted by monuments, gold Buddhas, enormous churches, gold chalices, which in many cases have been created at great cost, both human and material? How do you feel about this materialism in religion?

It is in the psychology of human beings to want to give our best to our divinity, to our god. All religions throughout history have developed and added, they have never subtracted: the tombs in Egypt, the Gothic churches in the Middle Ages, the emerald Buddha in Thailand... How do I feel? I believe that people need material symbols. People live with material and symbols. Symbols are expressed with or through materials, and man looks for the best material to express his symbols. It is a natural psychological tendency.

But Jesus was against these large temples. He would, I assume, have wanted to allocate the funds to feed and educate first.

There is no answer to that question, actually. It is man's nature. We form something, we want to perfect it. Let's say someone starts a company; he has an idea and says, "Okay, I have fifteen people, I want to do this." Then he says, "Oh, there is a possibility of this, also." So he expands. Expansion is a natural process. As for the religious...they want to expand, but their goal is to expand their belief. For this, they need people. They also need places for people to gather, and people are ready to give money. But not just money. You'd be surprised what people give to the church here. There is the Sunday collection, but you'd be surprised. A cake here, a shirt there. I received two shirts yesterday. Paul received two shirts. People are very kind. They want to give. So that is a kind of answer to your question.

Maybe I can give an example. This year was the fortieth anniversary of our church. The congregation wanted to do something special. They had a budget—a generous budget, which came from the donations by the congregation. I suggested a tabernacle, something that would remain in the church, for the church: for them. We have some members who are very wealthy—one member gave one fourth of the cost. We don't tell the community that this man gave this much. We never give this information. But people want to give. That, too, is in man's nature.

Very often, there are also collections for certain causes. We send a lot of money to Africa. We have some Dominicans there, and it is easier to send to people who know what the needs are. Caritas International is an organization that funds children, schools, and so on, run by the bishops who channel the money wherever in the world it is needed. In Turkey, two years ago, there was a huge earthquake, so after mass there was a special collection organized by lay committees. The pastor has to know, of course. Sometimes it happens in reverse, with the pastor making a suggestion, but everything is administered by lay people.

IV
THE COLLECTOR

It is not surprising that Gaston Petit is an enthusiastic traveller—many of the world's art treasures can only be seen on-site. Nor is it surprising that he is an art collector. What is less expected, perhaps, is that he reads Harry Potter and that he enters cooking competitions.

The Collector's Mania

In the tatami room of your atelier, I see some fine pieces of pre-Columbian art. Are you a collector?

Dangerous question. Don't get me started. Collectors can be fanatics. Once you start, collecting becomes almost compulsive. Controlling it takes a lot of willpower.

When I was still very young, I collected comic strips—part of my "art study." I was a bit of a magpie. I collected comic books, hockey cards, stamps and I don't know what else. Collecting stamps probably sparked my interest in geography, politics and history.

Once I arrived in Japan, I began to buy books that I needed for my courses—and others just for interest's sake. Then this other thing developed, my interest in objects. Once one begins, it becomes a real sickness.

I remember vividly the occasion when the collector in me was unleashed. It was at the beginning of the sixties. I used to meet with a group of expatriates to discuss the culture and the customs of the Orient. In fact, I was one of the co-founders of the Tokyo Ceramic Society. One of the collectors, I don't remember who, gave a lecture on the art of collecting. A good subject. I remember in particular a pair of ancient wooden ducks from Egypt, and two ceramic vases said to be Shawankalok of Thailand. He mentioned that certain museums, in Cairo, for example, sell objects—certified as authentic—because they have a surplus. Today, something like those fifteenth-century Shawankalok vases would still not be very difficult to find on the market at a reasonable price.

I was hooked. I found myself poking around here in Japan and on my many trips abroad.

The terracotta figurines you see in the tatami room—I am particularly fond of these. Except for a few from Java, they are all are pre-Colombian. The figurines and vases are from a catalogue of authentic objects I came across toward the end of the sixties. I sold most of the vases later, although I have kept a couple of good pieces. In my studio in Champlain, for example, I have a vase dated between 300 BC and 300 AD from Chupicuaro in

Gaston in front of the ten silkscreens composing the album Stigmates with a poem by Paul-Henri Girard, 1970.

the province of Guanajuato in Mexico. I'm a little sorry about a few of them that I sold, but I had to in order to pay for the figurines I kept.

You also had an important collection of Japanese prints, but today, the majority of them are part of the permanent collection of the British Museum in London. It seems what you have kept are primarily prints done by your students.

I parted from the Japanese prints because I had drawn what I could from them. I had studied them from every angle, for themselves, as art objects, but also to follow the development of the artists who had created them. I had reached an end.

It was the same with a collection of about thirty Inuit sculptures. I had spent some time with the Inuit at Povognituk, and after that, their sculptures, the form and the material, took on a new dimension for me, and I developed a deep interest. But one day, the life that had animated them disappeared. That life of an object arrives like a ray of sunshine and disappears, fades, more or less slowly. I don't know why. One could say that they had lived their life—for me.

On the other hand, I have kept some rather disparate objects: a Japanese Haniwa figure from the third or fourth century, ceramic Thai bowls from the fifteenth century, wooden Santos sculptures from the Philippines, fourth or fifth century pieces from Guatemala and Costa Rica, a few tiny ancient Egyptian figurines, ceramic shards collected on visits to various archaeological sites around the world... Some have sentimental value, but others have historical value. I should make a small catalogue. I just haven't had the time.

The British Museum: From the Collection of Gaston Petit

There is a collection of a thousand Japanese contemporary prints "From the Collection of Gaston Petit" at the British Museum. These prints were lithographs, silkscreen prints, mixed media prints, etc., ten or fifteen of which are prints that you did yourself. I can understand you being willing to give up your own work to the British Museum, but it must have been difficult giving up so much of your own private collection.

Not really. I had "used them up," the same way I had used up my collection of Inuit art. The collection was a result of the two books on prints that I wrote when I was teaching. My point was not to write about prints, actually, but to see how they had been made. Every artist mentioned in the book is someone I interviewed either here or in New York. Some Japanese artists were in New York at the time.

I needed a complete picture of each artist, his techniques, the material he used, work he had done in the past as well as the work he was doing: his development as a printmaker, in other words. Oftentimes we exchanged prints; others I bought. So I ended up with a rather substantial and complete collection which I used for demonstration with my students—look at this print, it was done this way using this kind of paper, this kind of material, this kind of ink. When I stopped teaching, I had them in my drawers for years, seldom looking at them because I had no time. I parted from them because at that point they meant nothing. I had emptied them, taken everything I wanted to take from them. They had became useless in a way. And so I offered them to different institutions, and the British Museum was eager. The British Museum had an extensive collection of Japanese Ukiye-o prints, prints of the Floating World (sixteenth century) to the beginning of the last century, the twentieth century, but for some reason, they had not pursued their collection. What I had really filled the void.

Have you ever seen your collection on display?

No, I haven't been in England since then. They have a huge selection of paintings, prints, sculptures, you name it, from all periods. Their shows go by theme or technique, so who knows if and when they are on view? Some day I'll go, maybe. It doesn't interest me, really.

The Mask, the Icon, and the Opera

The Noh mask is an image which appears over and over in your paintings and prints. You have a Noh mask, a very old, very worn mask, delicately perched on a ceramic paper bag in the bathroom of your atelier in Shibuya.

Real Noh masks are rarely found in the market—they are used in the theatres even if they are very old. So they are very worn, enriched with the patina of time—and enriched also with history. The only Noh mask I have, the one you refer to, comes from a small village near Nagano. It is sculpted in a very "artisan" way. It is adorable—even if it is etched by time and use. This is the little mask that you see in the *Geste de David* series. In a way, the rigid features of the Noh mask conceal a rare psychic force. It is like a moment of life captured in time.

So perhaps it is a question of availability. I was going to ask why you have so few Noh masks, while, on the other hand, I've seen several African masks on your walls, particularly in your studio in Champlain.

Yes, availability, and also, I remain fascinated by the African mask. In fact, I have acquired quite a few African masks, as well as small sculptures, over the years. I am not the first artist to be so fascinated by them. African masks were in the Trocadéro Museum in Paris long before the end of the nineteenth century, not as art so much as anthropology. Picasso saw them there and was blown away. He felt that they were more than the form of a mask, that they were infused with energy, that they were like a kind of *peinture exorcism*. He felt that some of these masks were magic, that they were intercessors, mediators.

Even in Europe at the beginning of the twentieth century, in general, art objects were made to be used, not to be exhibited and sold. In other words, works of art in Europe have changed status, from utilitarian objects to objects of trade, which has resulted in a certain alienation.

The mask is an object where sense and form are inseparable; the object, which is itself spirit, transmits aesthetic values and socio-cultural messages simultaneously. One cannot consider the mask without considering the society of masked dancers and the masquerade from which it has evolved. All ritual is a sacred drama. The domain of ritual is the sphere where the world of reality, the world of the five senses, and the world of image, or imagination, fuse, forming a single reality. In the case of the African rituals, when the dancer puts on his costume and the mask, he becomes a power which provokes a powerful emotional reaction among the spectators.

The specific contribution of the mask to the ritual is as personification of the spirits. The sculptor attempts to establish the connection between nature and man, between the individual and the society, between the present and the past, by reproducing the heroes of the mythic or legendary personalities, in detailing the sculptures which serve to evoke the spirits of the ancestors.

African masks are made more to be used than to be looked at, and they are imbued with spiritual strength. They have both a ritual and social utility. They are fetishes. Artists who make them are working for a particular social group. When I realized this, I had a new perspective on my own art. I was led to draw parallels between the inner meaning of African sculpture and what I do myself in my own culture.

For example?

What I have been doing in churches and in chapels for years is what I call religious art. In parallel with the artists of the African sculptures and masks, or even in parallel with the Haida artists of the west coast of Canada, I make objects that are more to be used than to be looked at. They are objects used in a ritual way, imbued with spiritual strength. In fact, when I do them, I have to dig deep into myself to find the right attitude—call it "vibes," "grace," "energy," what you will—of heart and mind to fabricate the objects which will answer their purpose, in effect, objects to be used for Christian rituals in Catholic churches—tabernacles, stations of the cross, the altar, the pulpit, the cross, stained glass windows. They are objects more to be used than to be looked at.

My feelings about my art, especially that part of my art which is done for church purposes, have been changing. I can say that my art production is moving slowly towards a different level of perception, towards a more spiritual meaning, maybe. I feel much less inclined now to make art for art's sake. What I mean by this is that I feel much less inclined to draw and to paint all the time, endlessly, as in the past, and less inclined to organize solo or group exhibitions. In brief, to exhibit, to be part of the art world. To keep my name out there. I won't object when asked to participate, but I will not come forward to organize exhibitions any more.

Has your health had anything to do with this change?

I don't think so. At this point, my health is very good, even if I no longer feel thirty years old. It is my perception of art that has changed. Somehow I feel that I am slowly drifting away from the world of exhibitions or art for art's sake to the world of function. I am more drawn by what I am doing in religious art, to use my own term, to make icons such as are found in Orthodox churches, if I can add another example of "used" art, as the African artists have made them. Maybe it is what I have

Champlain studio, 2000.

been called for. Not to say that I no longer have prints or paintings for sale—at twenty paintings produced sometimes in five days, you can imagine that some remain.

You think of the icons in Orthodox churches as similar to African masks, then, that they serve the same function.

What I mean is that both have some strong basic values in common: a ritual function, a religious function, and both are made more to be used than to be looked at.

Traditionally, icons for the Orthodox Church are the symbolic reflection of a superior spiritual truth. Icons are not the personal vision of the artist. Icons are at the same time art objects and cultural and ritual objects. As with African art, we know that icons are executed under very rigid rules with fixed styles and pre-established formulas expressing abstract symbols of another life. They do not depict human beings transformed as saints, but saints which conceal symbolic and distant human appearances. This perception of art is far from my own, but it is valid in itself. In the popular mentality, icons are thought of as the incarnation of the saint himself. The icon is affected by man's actions, just as are living beings. The icon can cry, become upset, punish, forgive. It can even die.

A point to remember is that icons were traditionally located in a special place in the house called the "red corner." Do icons have a contemporary relevance? I think of Malevitch and his famous painting *Black Square,* a totally sober work, a rejection of personal originality or any anecdote whatever that would interfere with contemplation. During an exhibition, Malevitch hung the *Black Square* in a high corner of the room, as an icon of old would have been, making an obvious link between the old icons and the new icon. He stressed the link a year later in 1961 when he said, "I have but one icon, bare and without a frame. It is the icon of my time." In its own way, *Black Square* is an icon that can be considered to be an object more to be used than to be looked at.

So you are retiring, in a sense, from the "public" art world.

It seems so. But maybe more taking a new direction. One never knows what comes one's way. For instance, I designed an opera. I love opera, but this is something I never expected.

Opera?

A Japanese friend of mine who is a serious opera lover asked me if I would be interested in designing an opera for a production in Korea. He was commissioning a rather unusual creation, a new Japanese-Korean opera, the music being composed by a Korean and the libretto written by a Japanese. The orchestra would be Japanese; the singers would come from both countries.

This is in keeping, before you ask, with my idea of "anonymous art," or my interest in art for the church—the story was inspired by the persecution of the Christians in Korea in the mid-nineteenth century. I envisioned the production, though, in a very modern way—seven very large television screens stacked in a kind of Greek cross to be placed in the centre of the stage. There would be slides projected, more than one thousand: abstract scenes, religious subjects, hands and faces... I also designed the costumes, chose the material, designed the three backdrops. I wasn't particularly satisfied with the result, actually. My television screens were cut, for instance, mostly for lack of money. I was at the premiere in Seoul on October 3, 1997, but I was truly the dissatisfied artist! I left before the end of the performance.

Agatha Christie, Harry Potter, and Strawberries with Black Pepper

Speaking of fascinations, I just finished reading the second Harry Potter book on the plane to Nagasaki. It was wonderful, delightful, enchanting. Everything the reviewers say about Rowlings is true. She is "splendiferous and delightful." What happened to your questions about the books I read? Did you cut it? Wasn't my answer interesting?

I'll put it back. Right now. I repeat: I see from your shelves in this wonderful studio apartment with stained glass windows and tatami that you have possibly several thousand books on art, history, art history, in French, English, Japanese—I also see Agatha Christie. Do you read mysteries?

More accurately, I read Agatha Christie. I discovered her at an airport. In fact, not long ago, I gave my superior a couple of Christie's books to read on his way to Rome. I found *Harry Potter and the Philosopher's Stone* on the bookshelf at the Dorval Airport in Montreal, and I now join thousands of children in dreaming of playing a Quidditch game on a Nimbus Two Thousand and One broomstick. I like the idea of being able to buy a flying broomstick, or at least a retractable broomstick, or even a self-stirring cauldron that would possibly make my dinner tonight. Unfortunately, it is not true that you can buy anything in Japan. Some things are not for sale. I did find, though, the second book, *Harry Potter and the Chamber of Secrets*, in a bookstore in Shibuya. I have two trips to make this month, and I will travel with Harry.

Are you also a collector of books?

Don't let the number of books fool you—when I buy a book, it is because I want to read it, not because I want to possess it. I am neither a bookmonger, a bookworm, nor a collector, even though there is also a certain sensuousness, a physical pleasure in letting your fingers move across the paper, sensing the coolness, the smoothness of glossy paper.

We put back one question for you. We're going to put one back for me. Your recipe for strawberries with black pepper, please.

Frankly, it has been a well-kept secret.

Fair is fair.

It's four or five strawberries per person, a couple of spoonfuls of sugar for the total, but not too much. Stir. A lot of ground pepper; tell your guests to tell you when to stop. Stir again. This will make the strawberries cry. But we do not want your guests to cry. Add Pernod and Grand Marnier to taste, again not too much. Stir. Pour heavy cream over the whole, and serve immediately.

As you have said yourself, artists are often very good cooks. I suspect it is because you are such a sensuous lot. You were once on national television cooking up the dish that won a bronze medal.

Cooking—oh, cooking. Yes, I love cooking. I love having people to dinner, good conversation. Conversation is an art as well.

This was when I was teaching. One of the students mentioned a competition that Kikkoman, of Kikkoman *shoyu*, soy sauce—we get it even in Canada—was organizing. I concocted chicken with a sauce containing the required Kikkoman *shoyu*, and I received a bronze medal along with a case of Kikkoman *shoyu*. You can imagine—twenty-four huge bottles of Kikkoman *shoyu*—I gave them away. Oh, yes, and a case of spaghetti sauce. The television crew came later: I was to cook my chicken dish, and would I please think of an additional recipe of my country, and some famous person would talk to me while I cooked.

What was the Canadian recipe you chose? That must have been difficult, considering our regions, the ethnic mix...

Une fricasée de poisson. A fish casserole, in other words. It is a dish we make in my region of Quebec between Christmas and the New Year when a small fish, only about twenty centimetres, runs in one of our rivers. Thick slices of potatoes, butter, pepper and salt, and white wine, and when the potatoes are almost baked, we place this small fish on top. Catching them in the Ste-Anne-de-la-Pérade River is winter entertainment, an all-night party. Fishing shacks with a small hole in one wall and without floors are placed on the ice. A string with ten hooks is dropped, and we wait, sitting on the ice with a small heater, refreshments. Attracted by the light in the shacks on the ice above them, the fish seize the hooks; we pull up the string, and the fish are thrown onto the ice outside through the hole. They freeze instantly. Since these delicate fish are not imported to Tokyo from my region in Quebec, and they do not run in the Tokyo rivers, I used cod. Voilà.

V
THE SHOES OF CAMELS

Ideas stick to the shoes of camels, an ancient proverb says, and even Japan, a seemingly isolated series of islands, embodies much of other ancient cultures. Spices, silks, philosophies, religions, art…there is a ceaseless ebb and flow. We see the "footprints" of Gaston Petit in his work as he has tracked some of these paths.

Cambodia: Angkor Wat (1964)

You visited Angkor Wat before the vandalism by the Khmer Rouge, did you not?

Yes, and I studied so much before I went there that a colleague asked, "Why bother going? You already know it so well." "Yes, I know it well enough," I said, "but now I want to really see it."

I was there in February 1964, not so long before the rise of the Khmer Rouge.

Oddly, the first thing I saw, just outside Siem Reap as I approached greater Angkor, was a cross. It was on the roof of a house that was a little more imposing than all the others. A church, I surmised. I stopped. The priest was Vietnamese; he spoke very good French, which was no surprise, since Cambodia had been colonized by France. I asked if he could put me up for a few days. He took me out back and showed me a square room on stilts, beneath which were pigs. As he climbed up the ladder ahead of me, he asked, "Do you prefer pigs or snakes?" "Pigs, of course." "Very good. You will not be bothered by snakes, as they won't come near the pigs." His hospitality, when he had so little himself, was very touching. He had just gotten himself a motorcycle, so he offered me his old Vespa to get around in.

When I arrived at the entrance to the temples, the young man at the gate also spoke French. He was a little cheeky: "But that is the car of Mr. Jesus Christ!" "It certainly is," I said. "Then for you, it is half price. But could you give me the other half for my little brother's education?" I was only there for a couple of weeks, so I have no idea if his brother was able to complete his studies.

The people were absolutely captivating, very simple, their faces always lit up with a smile. It is hard to imagine how this great calm could turn to carnage and murder a few years later.

You have spoken of a "belt of faith" between the eighth and the twelfth centuries, and you included Angkor in that belt.

Yes. The Khmers have a very long history—the first period of Khmer history is the first century to the middle of the sixth century, the Fou-nan period. The Angkorian period was from the ninth century when Angkor became the capital, and it remained the capital until the fifteenth century when for some reason the court abandoned Angkor and moved the capital to Phnom Penh. Phnom Penh, as you know, remains the capital. That's a quick summary of the history of the Khmers.

Angkor Wat, at the centre of Angkor, is both a temple and a tomb, is it not?

Exactly. It is both a classic temple, and a funeral temple. The tomb of the king, Vishnu. For the Khmer, a king had divine rights in life, and in death became a god. Angkor Wat is the most important of the Angkor complex, and the most imposing. It is the logical result of the temple-mountain which had evolved during the preceding centuries—one of the world's ancient Axis Mundi, if you remember an earlier conversation.

I'm going to quote something now. Turn off the machine. I have to find the book… Voilà. G. Coedès. *Pour mieux comprendre Angkor, Better Understanding Angkor.* Page 118. His explanation of the philosophy behind the architecture:

> "For the ancient Khmers, architecture and decoration were a language through which they expressed the pre-established harmony between the human and the divine, between our terrestrial world and the Great Whole. Their achievements are, above all, images, replicas, whose models we must understand if we are going to penetrate their thinking."

A detail. I have a collection of graphic documents of the Angkor Wat, the grand temple, some 113 plates, essentially architectural blueprints, on a scale of 1/50. I could actually reconstruct an exact model of Angkor Wat in my atelier.

Again. Page 87:

> "The reciprocal relationship between cosmology and architecture rests upon a concept of the world, which originated in the ancient Orient, of the belief in a magical relationship between microcosm and macrocosm, between humanity and the universe, between terrestrial manifestations on the one hand and the cardinal points and constellations on the other. Following this belief, the elements, colours, animals, the parts of the body and character, all events in life, age and sex, asceticism and pleasure, birth and death, living and dying are distributed among the areas of space and the stars which determine one's destiny, and all have their 'magic place' determined in the structure of the universe and their 'magic time' linked to the movements of the planets."

Hinduism has something similar—this is from Coedès also. I'll summarize: in the Brahmanic concept of the world a central continent, Jambudvîpa—at the centre of which rises a cosmic mountain, Meru, surrounded by planets—is encircled by six annular ring-shaped and concentric continents and seven oceans, the seventh of which is bounded on the outside by an enormous rock wall. At the summit of Meru Mountain is the villa of Brahma, the world of the gods, surrounded by the eight guardians of the cardinal points.

Let me quote from Coedès again.

> "The Buddhist system, so different in its details, also rests on the idea of a central mountain, Meru, over which rise the various skies. The two systems rest on the idea of a central mountain or a golden horn, the pivot of a world which is bound at its outer edge by a high wall plunging into the ocean."

Afghanistan: The Giant Buddhas of Bamiyan (1972)

I don't know if you are particularly attracted by giant art, or whether it's a case of historic sites being gigantic. You also visited the giant Buddhas at Bamiyan long before they were destroyed by the Taliban (in March of 2001).

Yes, destroyed on the pretext that they are idols, in spite of international protest. It is cultural sacrilege. One could argue that they were no longer idols. The faces of the sculptures had long ago been destroyed; it is an entirely Muslim country; it had been several centuries since any Buddhist ritual had taken place there. At this point, the giant Buddhas were Buddhist art representative of the past, the history of the country.

On the other hand, some people console themselves with the idea that destruction is part of the Buddhist philosophy.

Yes, I agree, nothing is permanent. But still—I saw them in the seventies. September, 1972. It was a good time. In the 1960s and right up to the middle of the 1970s, many places were still untouched, in their original state... There was no problem of access. This was Afghanistan before the Taliban, Iran in the time of the Shah, Ethiopia during the reign of Salassie...

The Buddhas are impossible to describe. Truly astounding. They had to be experienced. Although mechanized travel made it easier to get from Kabul to Bamiyan, which is 180 kilometres through the Unai and Hajigak passes, it still took more than six

Gaston outside yurt in Bamiyan, Afghanistan, 1972.

hours by car. I'll let you do the math to figure out our average speed. Roads weren't marked; they were narrow. We often had to act as both the lookout and guide to help figure out the route. The scenery was breathtaking. So were the heights, 3,250 metres. There was very little vegetation except alongside the rivers which wound through the bottoms of the valleys below us. Far below. Above us, geological formations on the mountain peaks looked like the ruins of ancient forts or castles. At one point, we stopped on a mountaintop and our driver, who could speak a smidgen of many languages, even Japanese, pointed out the Soviet Union on our left and China on our right, while we ourselves were in Afghanistan.

By the time we arrived at our first-class yurts—running water, showers, a veritable Hilton—on the plateau above the village of Bamiyan, night had fallen. The driver told us that we were invited to a wedding, so we followed him down a winding footpath to the village. We—only the men, of course—were herded into an interior court, where we sat leaning against a high wall. There were lamps and coloured garlands—it was very festive. Suddenly, everyone got up. We followed suit. The driver announced, "We are going back." So we went back, up the winding path in the dark.

All night long, about every fifteen or twenty minutes, there would be a piercing scream. You can imagine how much sleep we were getting. It was only in the morning that we learned what had been happening. On the other side of the wall behind us, there had been a fight. Someone had been stabbed. The prison guard didn't want to fall asleep, so he screamed to keep himself awake.

But that morning, I opened the little curtain of my yurt, and there they were, the huge Buddha sculptures in a high cliff across the valley, like an apparition, as if projected on a giant screen. We set off by car right after breakfast. They rose before us like Titans.

The Buddhas are carved into the cliff, in kind of niches. They have been faceless as long as anyone can remember. The large Buddha is at least fifty-three metres high, the smaller one a mere thirty-five metres. The draped robes were made with wooden forms hammered into the rock and covered with a mixture of mud and straw. From the vestiges of colour, it seems that the Buddhas had been painted. It is said, though there is no evidence of it, that their faces and their hands were covered with gold. It is also said that at the base of the sculptures there were once stupas and other kinds of constructions. Hsan-Tsang, a Chinese pilgrim, reported in 632 AD that more than a thousand monks were living in Bamiyan. There are still hundreds of caves in the cliffs that were used as living quarters. In some of the caves, there are frescoes—faded, fragments—which seem to have been painted by Indian and Iranian artists. They can easily be compared to the paintings of Sassanide, Gupta and even Ajanta. These are no doubt gone as well.

From the techniques used to construct the Buddhas, it would seem that they date from the second and third century of our era, a period which corresponds to the worship of colossal idols in the Roman Empire as well. Some say that there was an influence—ideas on the shoes of camels.

It is terrible to see what the Taliban have done to the Buddhas of Bamiyan. But art, religious art, is often the target of despots and fanatics. Look at what the Khmer Rouge did at Angkor Wat and the Angkor temples.

The Drawings in the Nazca Desert (1972)

You travelled to Peru to see the giant drawings in the Nazca Desert. What was your reaction—the artist's reaction?

I went first to Lima, which is a very dusty city, but the avenue connecting the two piazzas had a good collection of ancient pottery, and good cafés. I remember getting vertigo in the gloomy church court where the heretics had been tried, and the huge black cross at the end of the room.

Then to Cuzco, which is at an extremely high altitude. I had terrible nausea—altitude sickness, lack of oxygen. The hotel concierge gave me a drop of a magical transparent liquid—I have no idea what it was, but within minutes the nausea disappeared. Finally I went even higher to lose myself in the clouds of Machu Picchu, an altitude of 2,500 metres. This time, no problem.

I flew from Lima to Nazca, a very strange desert. You can see enormous lines, sort of geometrical tracks, a hundred spirals and zoomorphical drawings spread out over 500 square miles of desert pampas. It never really rains—there is never a thundershower, never a storm—so they are preserved. No one knows how old these drawings are, perhaps 2,000 years, perhaps 3,000. It is one of the most enigmatic archeological sites on earth.

All sorts of hypotheses have been advanced to explain these drawings.

Yes—from landing strips for mysterious flying men, to choreographic patterns of an erotic fertility cult, to observatories of a magico-religious sect for programming the future, to ramps for launching hot air balloons to transport the corpses of nobles to their final resting place, and I don't know what all else.

A plausible explanation would be that the birds, the fish, the monkey, the spider, the lizard, the dog, and the llama were made kilometres long so that the gods could see them from their heavenly heights. In other words, the drawings were representations laden with ritual supplication to attract the attention of the gods. Or, according to another theory, these drawings would be seen by the souls of the dead chiefs of the clan as they made their way to the great ocean by way of hot air balloons. They were the only ones who could or would ever see them. Can you imagine the kind of imagination—the faith, the dedication—to work on something that you could never ever see? I saw them from an airplane, just the pilot and me, buckled in very tightly because there was no door. We spent almost an hour diving down to look at the drawings, then climbing vertically again. I could only take an hour—I was so airsick I had to ask him to land.

It is impossible to understand the shapes if you don't see them from above. High above. It is impossible to appreciate the grace, the realism, the proportions, and the amazing precision of these huge stylized creatures. I know of no other place on earth where you have to be up in the air to observe a man-made construction. There are more than 200 monumental figures: birds with cocked legs which appear to be hedge-hopping, their wings and tails majestically deployed—the radius of the heads of the largest of them are between ten and twenty metres; there is a dog leaning on his paws; a large maquisapa monkey with only four fingers drawn in an unbroken line which ends with a series of seven zigzag lines; the superb spider, a real work of art.

With the aerial view, you can see a curious system of deliberate patterns or repetitions. There are innumerable long straight lines, almost all of which are crossed by one or several other diagonal lines, often with a parallel groove, a furrow, underscoring it. Some of the parallel lines are doubled. Others go in a zigzag or a combination wavy line. There are hundreds of triangles, and elongated quadrangles, and trapezoids.

It would have taken thousands of hours, several generations, to execute the lines and drawings.

I had an odd experience there. It was like something from de St. Exupéry's *The Little Prince*.

Picture it. I am on the desert, no one but me and drawings that are kilometres long. In the distance, I see a figure. As I get closer, I see it is a small woman with white frizzy hair and skin as pale as parchment.

Her name was Maria Reiche, and she was a scientist. She had come from Germany to Peru in 1932. By the time I met her that day, she had spent just over forty years, from 1946, doing research on Nazca. I have her book, a small book, with a sand-coloured cover: *Mystery on the Desert, Secreto de la pampa.* I bought it from her later, and she dated it the day we met on the desert. She may still be there.

Were you able to discern how these figures were "drawn"?

Yes, and I would say that the method was as arduous as it was simple—by clearing and cleaning the black topsoil to expose the ochre ground beneath. Millions of tons of soil and pebbles would have been removed. What is still a mystery is what original "drawing pen" or plumb line, what slide rule or what T-square, compass, square or kilometric protractor could the Nazcas have used to draw these mega-drawings? How did they manage to draw that beautifully, perfectly proportioned spider? It is impossible from the ground, if you are near the insect's head, to make out the enormous globular body, and even more difficult to see the limits of the long legs, so at no point could they have viewed their work in its entirety. Aside from all the other mysteries in this, it is truly a mystery of art.

Easter Island, 1978.

Easter Island: The Moaîs (1972)

After the vast desert drawings in Nazca, and the complexity of Angkor Wat, Easter Island must have been a totally different experience.

Absolutely. An absolutely tiny island. It astonishes me that the original Polynesian inhabitants found the island at all. Imagine an isosceles triangle with a base of twenty-five kilometres and two equal sides of about eighteen kilometres. At each of the angles there is an extinct volcano, with steep eroded slopes. Between the volcanoes is a green plain and just enough space for a short runway. A wild and dramatic scene. The sheep outnumber the people, although there are a few more people than statues. There is a single village, Hanga Roa, where the approximately 1,500 inhabitants live. Place this tiny island in the middle of the Pacific, 2,700 kilometres from Chile and 4,000 kilometres from Tahiti. There is an odd timelessness about this place.

Thor Heyerdahl, the famous Swede of the Kon Tiki expedition, wrote a massive book on the expedition. He wanted to prove that the Pascuans could have arrived on the island this way, and he proved it by doing it himself. The expedition went from Polynesia to Easter Island. Much of the book is about Easter Island itself. The size of the book is in inverse proportion to the size of the island. He will also tell you that in the local language, Easter Island is Te-Pito-O-Te-Henua.

The story goes that, arriving from Polynesia on their rafts, along with their chickens, their edible rats, bananas, sugar cane and sweet potatoes, the Polynesian immigrants multiplied until they reached a critical mass of 10,000, at which time, the island being unable to support such numbers, they became cannibals. Man hunted man and then ate him. There was fratricidal warfare between the Long Ears, the old ones, and the Short Ears, the recently arrived. The building of *moaîs* stopped. Two or three thousand inhabitants survived, but from then on, they lived in the many underground caves. On December 12, 1862, about 1,000 years later, another calamity. A Peruvian flotilla dropped anchor in the Hanga Roa harbour. They enticed the Pascuans with cheap trinkets, then took them prisoner and deported them to Peru to work in the mines, where almost all of them died. By 1870 there were only 111 inhabitants left. All the tribal chiefs and all those who were familiar with the oral and written traditions had died, and the secrets of their civilization died with them.

All that remains, essentially, are the *moaîs,* these mysterious and majestic sculptures placed all around the island on the seashore with their backs to the sea. The victors had knocked down the *moaîs* of the defeated, of course, so not all are standing. The statues are six to ten metres in height, the largest, dating from around the sixth century, weigh an estimated twenty-four tons. In fact, they are nothing but short, legless trunks, with stylized arms, and hands with elongated fingers. The bones, the remains of the ancestors, were buried beneath these sculptures. It was as if the ancestors could look out through the eyes of the sculptures, watching over their progeny.

I saw a great many sculptures at every stage of fabrication. Most of them were hewn from a quarry on the slopes of Rano Raraku volcano. To scale the mountain you must climb over the bodies, like a stairway of Titans, grabbing hold of a nose here, an ear there. They all seemed to be using the same model, with a very long nose, a small mouth, a square chin, and large holes for very wide-open eyes. They are dressed in a kind of collarless tunic, carved out of the stone, with a round red stone on their heads that reminded me of the hats worn by the Russians or by Hassidic Jews. Some of them were finished and standing upright, ready to be delivered; others were lying down, carved completely out of the mountain; and still others had been barely started.

One of the mysteries of Easter Island is how a twenty-four-ton statue would have been transported from the quarry to the site where it was erected.

It isn't known for certain what technique was used. The most plausible theory comes from Thor Heyerdahl: that the sculptures were dragged along, pivoting on themselves, and then raised slightly with long hoists of wood and rope, while at the same time larger and larger rocks were slid beneath until they were completely upright. Heyerdahl had eight Pascuans install a *moaî* in just this way. It took them exactly twelve days.

Ideas Stick to the Shoes of Camels (1989)

Much of the travel has been related, as you put it, to your artistic education. The Silk Road, though, doesn't fit that category. If you follow the whole route from Istanbul to Xi'an, it is thousands of

kilometres. It must have taken weeks. What drew you to this?

I suppose it was a fascination with the adventurous spirit, the almost superhuman effort required. When I was studying Asian cultures at Sophia University at the beginning of the 1960s, the Silk Road, the traffic and trade, was one of my favourite subjects. In fact, there were a number of routes running parallel to each other, but two thousand years ago, no matter which route you took, it was by horse, by camel, and on foot. There weren't just endless deserts, enormous mountain ranges, savage streams—there were also barbarians and thieves. Just imagine how many must have lost their lives, and all for the very practical purpose of trading goods.

You mean making money.

Yes. But what interested me was the exchange of ideas. There is a saying in the Middle East: ideas stick to the shoes of camels. The Silk Road connected two great empires of the time, the Roman Empire and the Chinese empire. One example is religion. Christianity came into being in the Near East, but took the western direction, and today it is the main religion of the West. Buddhism was born in Nepal, but by the sixth century was flourishing in Japan. It travelled east along the Silk Road on the shoes of those camels, across the deserts and the mountains, and took an extra leap over the sea.

With mechanized means of transportation, today the Silk Road is much easier to travel, but it is still far from relaxing. I went in 1989; there were fifty-

On the Silk Road. Baseklik, between the Gobi and the Taklamakan deserts, 1989. Above the Murtuk River Gorge there are sixty-seven caves, The Thousand Buddha Caves, dating from the fourth to the fourteenth century.

Gaston with Chinese soldiers on the Silk Road. Yining, China, 1989 .

two of us from twelve different countries. We travelled by train, by buses large and small, on all kinds of roads. Hotel accommodation was, shall we say, varied. Sometimes it was whichever vehicle we happened to be in. The food was adequate, although there was often a shortage of potable water. In countries as hot as some of these can be, a shortage of drinking water is not comfortable.

And your next trip?

I'd like to bring myself up to date. I do it to some extent by reading, but I dream—it's good to dream—that one day I'll be able to revisit all the places I've been. I also dream that I will visit new sites as well. There are articles in newspapers and magazines constantly about new archeological discoveries. There have been some recent discoveries in Peru, north of Lima, the Moche tombs. A civilization of unknown origin lived there a few thousand years before the Incas and disappeared completely. The world is full of mysteries, not just philosophical mystery.

Culture Shock & Near Misses

During all your travels, have you ever experienced culture shock?

I'd say I've experienced serious culture shock twice. The first time was when I arrived in Japan in 1961. It was my first time travelling abroad, and, certainly, Japan was a jump into the unknown. It was not to be unexpected. I mentioned the shock of the dinginess.

The second shock was when I arrived in Calcutta in 1964, after having gone through vibrant Hong

Kong, Cambodia and Angkor Wat with its grand structures and its mix of Buddhism and Hinduism, and Thailand which I thought was still like a Siam of yore, so full of life and dripping with gold. But Calcutta—the heavy heat, the indescribable filth, and the appalling poverty, was practically intolerable. Children, often purposely crippled—missing limbs, for instance—would cling to you like flies, desperate for a few pennies. *Baksheesh! Baksheesh!* It still rings in my ears.

What I really wanted to do was escape, but I had arrived with a goal. I wanted to visit Varanasi, the ancient Benares. I felt completely lost, helpless, in this motley mob; it was nauseating and repulsive—a spectacle of distress. It was only because of the kindness of a rickshaw driver that I was able to continue. He took me in hand, protected me, guided me. Otherwise, I think my courage would have failed—but I went on to the extraordinary temples of Bhubaneshwar, Santchi, Mahavalipuram, Madurai, Ellora, Ajanta and I don't know how many others, completely relaxed. His kindness—it had an eloquence beyond words.

Tula, Mexico, 1968.

I've had experiences impossible to describe—Pagan in Burma, Myanmar today, thousands of temples spread over a great desert plain under a sapphire blue sky, the sunset behind red stone and bleached white stone structures. The splendid Islamic archictecture of central Asia, the blue mosaic cupolas. Isfahan, Buhkan, Samarkand, the palace of Registan…

How about near misses, a feeling of, "Oh-oh, maybe I should have stayed home"?

Probably more than a few. Two stand out, though, both on the same trip, in 1978. The first was in Isfahan in Iran. I was strolling with my camera through the many turquoise-domed mosques glittering in the intense light. There were two of us, Paul-Henri Girard, a Dominican colleague, and I. We were admiring the splendid cupolas of some mosque or other when the guard offered to unlock the door for us to go up inside the minaret. We'd had plenty of very specific warnings: "You are infidels; do not be seen in a minaret." In the face of the offer to actually go in, though, all advice flew out of our heads.

So there we were, mounting the narrow spiral staircase, holding on to the wall in the darkness, which, after the brilliant sun, was pitch black. Every once in a while there was a tiny window for air circulation, but they let in precious little light.

When we reached the top, all the glazed tile domes were laid out before us—what a view! And while we were admiring this view, Paul suddenly remembered the warnings. He was paralysed with fear: "What if the guard won't open the door to let us out?" We were the infidels, no way around that, and on top of the warnings, I had educated myself through books like Peter Hopkirk's *The Great Game*. Watkins describes the Muslim character as authoritarian, unyielding, not very conciliatory, and not open to concession. Heads have rolled for less. But with a bravado I was not really feeling, I announced, "Then I will go back up, and the citizens of Isfahan will hear a very original version of the Koran."

Fortunately, the guard did let us out, so the good citizens of Isfahan were saved.

And another stereotype bit the dust. The second?

The second was during the same trip on the way from Sri Lanka to Turkey. We had a number of stopovers in Arab countries, although I wasn't really paying attention to which countries they were, since we were merely in transit. All of our flights had been confirmed, so as far as I was concerned, there was nothing to worry about. We flew out of Colombo at 2:00 a.m. and arrived at the Dharan airport at 4:00 a.m. The airport was completely rundown, and the customs office was nothing but a desk in a hangar. The officer looked at our tickets and passports, and issued an order: "Sit down over there." It was clear that he had no intention of giving us our passports or our tickets back, and when I asked why or what we were expected to do—no response. So we sat on a wooden bench, not moving, keeping an eye on the cubicle that was the office, our tickets and our precious passports now sitting unattended on a small table. A dozen employees, one after the other, asked us who we were and where we were going, and we told them, one after the other, the same thing: "We live in Japan and are on our way to Canada, but we are stopping off on the way. Right now we are en route to Turkey." There were no amenities to speak of: no restaurant where you could get a coffee, no toilets in sight, nothing.

Around 10:00 a.m., six hours after our arrival (still no coffee, no breakfast), we were politely informed that we were to move our baggage elsewhere, and we were to follow the armed guard who had presented himself before us holding a large brown envelope which we hoped contained our

Sarnath, near Varanasi, India, 1961.

Persopolis, Iran, 1972.

tickets and passports. We followed him. We had no choice. A commercial plane was waiting on the tarmac, engines running.

I kept my cool, but I didn't dare think about anything except getting on the plane and getting out of Saudi Arabia. I'd never even heard of such a procedure for passengers in transit, and I was not an unseasoned traveller. As soon as we were seated I asked the steward to verify that the pilot did indeed have our documents. He did. Again, we were served nothing on the flight.

In less than two hours we landed in Jiddah, but I had now been up for ten hours and still had not had my morning coffee. As we deplaned by the first-class exit—evidently this was first-class treatment—the steward announced cryptically, "We no longer have any responsibility for you," and sent us off in the custody of a moustachioed gorilla-like guard, this one unarmed, carrying that brown envelope. He gestured us into a jeep, and we raced down the runway. By this time, I was so dispirited that I couldn't even appreciate the splendid white airport that seemed to float on the desert sands.

Although, from the way you describe it, you saw it. Evidently you can worry and see at the same time. And then?

We were taken into an office where an employee shouted, "Are you the Canadians?" and then we were put in the hands of another guard, this one armed. This was not feeling good. We were led this way and that through beautiful polished marble corridors, and—lo and behold—to the Turkish Air Lines office. The tickets and passport came out of the envelope, and were redone—why, we still didn't know. When we went through customs, a little rosette was stuck at the top of the folder: "Keep this until your departure."

We were now very politely taken to an extremely modern room with all the modern facilities for passengers in transit. Finally—breakfast and coffee. I began to relax. Two hours later, we were transported by bus to the plane. At the door, one of the ground staff removed the little rosette and said in French, "Bon voyage."

The Tri-star began to fill up with moustachioed Turks who had just completed their pilgrimage to Mecca and were as happy as children. In the meantime, I was still wondering what had transpired in the past twelve hours, but it wasn't until we were in the air that I felt secure enough to ask. According to the Turkish stewardess it was this: both Dharhan and Jiddah were in Saudi Arabia, and we didn't have visas. Yet we had to cross the country. Voilà.

When all is said and done, the authorities dealt with the problem admirably. It all happened as if had been on a magic carpet. We hadn't left a trace.

VI
THE PRIME MINISTER AND THE PRINCE

Life's circumstances can lead to odd coincidences: so it is that Gaston Petit came to lead a contingent of Japanese artists and art critics on a tour through Canada. And so it was that it was in Japan that the friendship with Canadian Prime Minister Jean Chrétien was forged. It is hard to remember, sometimes, that Gaston Petit the artist also has a life as a Dominican.

You and Prime Minister Jean Chrétien went to school together. Have you maintained a friendship since then?

We were acquaintances at that point—in the same class for a while, talking a little, but we lost track of each other. I went into the Dominican Order; he went on to law. I knew he'd gone into politics, that he had become the Minister of Justice. I was in Japan, I was in the Order, doing art, studying, teaching—I didn't pay much any attention to politics except when I heard rumblings about separatism.

What was your reaction?

You have only to look at my print, *Mon Pays, My Country, the Fleur de Lys and the Maple Leaf.* I feel Canadian. I don't say I am only Québécois. Canada has given me a great deal, a good education—my life, actually. I have a feeling of debt to my country. Like you. You tell people you are Canadian, but that you are from Saskatchewan.

Yes. True. My personal geography is the Saskatchewan prairie, although I definitely call myself Canadian. I think when you have been outside of the country as much as you and I have, we know more about what being Canadian means, and what there is to be proud of.

So you are in Japan. Jean Chrétien is in Ottawa as Minister of Justice. How did you reconnect?

Somebody from the Canadian Embassy told me one day that the Minister of Justice was coming, but only for three days. Naturally, I wanted to see him, another boy from Shawinigan (we were both born there) after all, doing well, who I hadn't seen since high school.

So I called the ambassador, Barry Steer. "Barry," I said, "I want to meet the Minister of Justice."

He was a bit taken aback, but he was very diplomatic: "He's very busy. He's coming on official business."

"I know."

Jean Chrétien, Aline Chrétien and Gaston.

"Well, we don't know his schedule…" More diplomacy.

I put him out of his misery. "We went to school together."

"Why didn't you say so in the first place! I'll check his schedule."

He called back the next day: on the last evening, there would be a reception for the Minister of Justice at his residence—the ambassador has a very elegant residence, as you know—so why didn't I come?

We queued up—you know how they line up to meet people—I recognized Jean; he recognized me—we were talking, and the line was getting backed up.

"People are waiting to meet you, Honourable Minister."

"Don't go away, I want to talk with you again. Why don't we have dinner together?"

"I would be honoured, my Honourable Minister of Justice!"

"Shut up!"

We had dinner at a French restaurant at his hotel. We talked about the past, what had happened to this student and that student. We never talk politics. I know nothing about politics, anyway. At 2:00 a.m., we were kicked out.

I could see the resilience of that man at that time, both physically and psychologically. After all, he

Stained glass master Matsumoto, Princess Hisako and Prince Takamado with Gaston viewing stained glass design, 1986.

had had only two or three days for a heavy schedule, with no time to recover from jet lag, and he was bubbling all the time.

Since then, every time he's come here, and every time I go back to Canada, we meet at least once, lunch or dinner together, sometimes in Ottawa, sometimes at their home on Lake Harrington. Once we went fishing together.

Well, to be accurate, he fished. I had stayed overnight, and in the morning, he said, "Do you like fishing?" "No." "You'll come just the same." He is the only one allowed to fish, so you can imagine how the lake jumps with fish. He would pull out a fish, and I'd say, "Too small." He would release the fish, cast the line, and pull out another fish. "Too small." For a good hour or two, he was catching fish, and they were all too small.

Does the Prime Minister have any of your paintings?

Many. Paintings and prints. He has a good collection. Before he became Prime Minister, every time we met, he bought something. But as Prime Minister—it is difficult.

How did Prince Takamado, the Emperor's cousin, come to know of your work? Did he attend one of your exhibitions at the Canadian Embassy?

No, this was long before any exhibitions at the embassy. He came to an exhibition at a private gallery, and bought *Mon Pays, My Country*. He and the Princess have drawings, and a few other prints, as well. I don't think they have any paintings.

And was it at this point that the Prince and Princess commissioned you to do a stained glass window for their new home?

Yes, actually, it was. It was very simple. The prince said, "I'm building a new home, and I would like to have stained glass windows from you." I said what you would expect. "Okay. Thank you."

No, I wouldn't expect your response to be that simple, not with the twenty-one levels of politeness, and a prince being at the top of the levels.

Perhaps not that simple. Even if I did not have the correct level, as foreigners, we are forgiven lapses. No one expects us to know all these levels. At any rate, in general, the Japanese don't believe we are capable of learning all the levels.

Did you feel pressure because the commission was coming from the royal family?

No, but to myself I said, "We'll see how this works out." There is not only a prince, but also a princess, and a whole imperial household who oversee and make many of the decisions. Royalty, as you know, does not usually have much freedom.

How involved were the Prince and Princess in the process?

Very. They were very interested in the entire process. The Prince was asking about technique from the first conversation at the opening, so I suggested that he come to the studio with the Princess before they made a decision. In the meantime, I was given the blueprints, and I taped off my studio floor in direct proportion to their living room, the entrance, and the stained glass window. The architect had left a square in the middle of the wall, but I thought that I would make a vertical slit facing the entrance. During the day, it would light both the corridor and the room, and the changing light of the sun would create a changing tableau; it would catch the light from the sunset: people would see it and turn, but they wouldn't be distracted by a square in the middle of the wall. They both seemed to go along with my suggestion, but the Prince said he would call the next day. He did: "The people of the

Imperial Household want to meet you." I got cold from here to here. But I had the intuition to tell them to come here to the studio. My home. Very different from going to an office.

On the appointed day, on the exact second, the doorbell rang. Two men were standing there, very correct, very erect. I placed them at this table, one opposite me where you are sitting, another at the end. I did not offer tea.

Question one: "You asked the Prince to change the location and proportion of the stained glass window."

I said, "I'm sorry, I *suggested* to the Prince"—we have to be very careful of our words—"it could be better for his room for these reasons."

"You want the window sixty centimetres from the inside wall. Could it be sixty-three centimetres instead of sixty?"

"No objection."

They had ordered tile to be made for the outside wall, and at sixty it would have meant a break in the tile. At sixty-three it would fall exactly on the tile.

One for him.

Second question: "The opening for this stained glass window goes from floor to ceiling. Seen from the outside, all the other windows are at the same height. Would you object to creating a balustrade on the outside wall to underline the level of the windows?"

"If you build a balustrade, it will definitely cast a shadow on the floor of the room, and I am sure that the Prince wouldn't like to have an unspecified shadow on his floor."

One for me. One-one. Very elegantly said. A dance.

The dance over, I offered coffee, which they accepted—I have excellent coffee from beans I buy and have ground at a shop up the street—and we had a good chat.

When the glass was cut and laid out on the table at the glass factory and ready for leading, I called the Prince to see if they were interested in coming with me to make the corrections.

"Definitely."

They picked me up. The Prince was driving, but we were followed by his bodyguards. He and the Princess saw the work that was being done, they had questions…and they offered to drive me home. It occurred to me that perhaps it was not necessary to be driven home by a prince, so I told them they could drop me anywhere, and I'd make my way home on my own.

A Day in the Life of a Dominican

We've talked about your life as an artist, but we haven't talked about your life as a Dominican. Can you describe a typical day?

Yes, but remember, in some ways there is no typical day for a Dominican, since one of us teaches at Tokyo University, I do art…

You do perform baptisms, funerals and marriages, though; at the ambassador's dinner when you were given the citation for your contribution to Japan/Canada relations in art I seem to remember meeting a couple you had married in Japan twenty-five years before.

As chaplain in Canada I had the same duties as a secular priest—that is, as a priest not attached to an order. The duties of a religious person are different, as I mentioned previously. If a church is attached to a convent, as we have here in Shibuya, it is to facilitate a community to practice their faith. May I add that parochial work is not the main purpose of the Order.

So, you want my day as a Dominican. At 7:30 a.m. there is mass, followed by the recitation of psalms and prayers. The others have breakfast together, but I have it here, toast, cereal. I am not an introvert, as you know, but I need balance. I need my time alone.

Mid-morning, I do the rounds of the entire building. This is new since I was elected prior a year and a half ago (November 2000). As prior, I am the superior responsible for the convent—the kitchen, the laundry, the smooth running of the entire operation. The buck stops here, as we say. I like order, so I don't like to see things left in corridors, shoes outside the door, for example. They must be inside the room. If I see things in disorder in the common rooms, books, and so forth, I put them back, but later there is a reminder.

Lunch is preceded by prayers, so at 12:15 there is about fifteen minutes of prayer and psalms. After lunch we gather in the communal room to chat. So even during the meals or after, we can settle small problems. In the evening, there is another time of prayer at about 6:30, followed by supper, and then at 10:00, for fifteen minutes, an unofficial gathering. On Sunday, the schedule changes slightly because of parochial activities. Often I'm out for dinner, or away for a day or two. Today, for instance, you and I went for lunch together.

In a few weeks, I have a lecture on art at the Rotary Club. That is also part of my "day" as a Dominican.

Entering the church, 1997.

So you still accept invitations to lecture. I assume, then, that you still enjoy it.

Good question. This is another "nyes." Preparing a lecture, and giving it, is work, even though I am not shy. I have been giving public lectures since 1970 when I had an exhibition in the Philippines. I was invited to do a series of lectures—thirty years ago, I barely remember which colleges: out of the five or six, only Santo Tomas University and Lasalle College come to mind. What I spoke about reflected what I was actually involved in—contemporary Japanese printmaking, children's drawing, my own artistic production, etc. Towards the end of the 1970s I gave another series of lectures on contemporary Japanese printmaking and the development of my own work at three Canadian universities: Queen's University in Kingston; the University of Regina in Saskatchewan; and the University of Victoria in British Columbia. I use slides, of course, which always makes any subject about art more interesting. Even for me. Sometimes the audience is particularly interesting. I lectured to an organization of bankers on the art market a few years ago. They were an interesting group. They knew nothing about the art market. Plenty about stocks, but nothing about art.

This is your first term as prior. Have you enjoyed it?

In the past I have been assistant to the prior, as well. Enjoyed? Yes, of course, it is a new challenge. I have to cut back on some of my usual activities—that is, my artistic activities, but I have received so much from the Order. If I can give back a little, why not?

This year has been heavy because of the arrival of five new novices, so we have been thirteen in total. The life of the convent has had to adapt to the fact that all five are people at various stages of their Dominican apprenticeship. We have to teach them the rules of religious life in detail, Dominican history, Dominican spirituality—everything that concerns the Dominican way of life. Two of the fathers are in charge of the novices' training, but in fact the whole community participates. And then we also often have visitors coming through, and that requires additional attention—both to the visitor and to matters related to welcoming them: making sure the room is ready, informing the kitchen…

Exactly one month from today, the 6th of March, the novices will take their first vows. Some who belong to the Spanish group will go, others will remain. Next year, there will be other novices coming.

You have been living separately, though, in your studio. Is there any resentment from the others as to what might be perceived as special treatment?

No, no resentment. As Dominicans, we are each to find our own way to teach, to preach, to search for the truth, but we go where we are called. Father Girard, for example, who has been in Japan even longer than I have, has lived in Fukushima, in Koriama, in Kyoto, and I have stayed here. Since I had to build a studio, I had to remain here. I am fixed because of that.

I did not arrive with the intention of making my way in art, remember. This was an organic process. There was a need, and the opportunity—I filled it. The first year, the church needed the stained glass windows designed, but really, for the first three years, I was studying the language, Asian culture, calligraphy, *sumi-e*. After three years, I did my first design of the chapel in Kyoto, then I took a leave of absence to go to Europe. It was when I came back in 1965 that I built the studio to work full-time.

Gaston in Shawinigan, September 1998.

The Seven Samurai

At the dinner held for you in 1999 at the ambassador's residence when you were awarded the citation for your contribution to Japan/Canada relations in art, one of the guests, the director of the Ikeda Museum of Twentieth Century Art in Ito, talked about the Seven Samuari and a trip you organized across Canada for art critics and museum directors—which included him. There was also reference, from the ambassador, I think, to the number of artists who had showings in Japan as a result of that trip.

The Seven Samurai. Yes. That was in 1976, I think, or 1977. The Canadian Embassy wanted to develop a program of cultural collaboration between Canada and Japan, but they weren't sure what to do. I had organized two exhibitions, one was of five Canadian printmakers in a gallery in Tokyo, and a second of ten Canadian printmakers. This one toured six or seven cultural centres throughout Japan and ended at the Fuji TV gallery here in Tokyo, a very prominent gallery. It was quite a success, I think. The cultural attaché asked me whether they should do something similar, hold an exhibition of Canadian artists, not just printmakers, or what. I thought it might be better to sensitize people who were in the field, critics, museum people, writers on art. One thing led to another and I was asked to organize a group to take on tour through Canada, to art museums, to galleries, to meet artists.

I was to choose six people. The majority I knew personally, but there was one person in the field of art, Seigi Junichi, who would be close to eighty now, who helped me. He was sort of an *eminence grise*: he had all the connections; he knew everyone. If he said, "You should go," the person would go.

Gilles, maman Antoinette and Gaston, 1986.

One was the director of the Fuji TV gallery. Kiichiro Hayashi, the one who spoke of the trip, is the director of the Ikeda Museum of Twentieth Century of Art in Ito. Yamamoto now is the director of the Fuji TV gallery. Not then, but now. Another is still with the *Asahi* newspaper. Miki Tamon is rather ill now, but he was at one time the director of a museum at Osaka, then he came back to Tokyo to the Harajuku museum of photography, I was told. Another was a critic. I don't know what has happened to him. He has totally disappeared.

We went from Vancouver to Banff, to Regina, to Winnipeg, to Toronto—not Niagara Falls—to Montreal. Toronto and Montreal were the main places, actually. We visited artists in their homes and in their studios to get a feel for the life of a plastic artist in Canada. Snow was in Toronto. He plays in a jazz trio. One of the members of his trio was a *nisei*, second generation Japanese. We went to the club one night to hear them. There was also Rita Letendre and her husband, Kosso Elul, a sculptor who has since died, whom we visited in their home. With such a high-energy group, you can imagine. The Seven Samurai take Canada. The appellation didn't come from me, actually. It came from someone else in the group.

The two-week trip was organized by Canada, so it was red carpet all the way: there was not a single flaw, and as a result, The National Gallery in Ottawa organized a huge exhibition of Canadian art that went to Sapporo, Fukuoka, and Tokyo. The trip had caused a buzz in Japan, so when the show came, critics and museum directors in Japan already knew about some of the work. There was a feeling of "we know—we are not writing about nothing." There was some excitement around the show.

But as for which artists came, I don't really know who or where. Doors were opened for them, and some organized their own shows here through the contacts that they had made. Canada gives artists grants to travel outside of the country. But I did not organize exhibitions myself.

May to October

For the last ten years or so, you have been spending the winters here in Japan, and going back to Canada for the summer, from May to October. What prompted this? What was it in Canada that you felt you were missing?

It was more a question of balance than of "missing." I was turning sixty. I was starting to feel a need to relax a little, and the tiny village of Champlain was the solution; the yin and the yang of my life. The very active life in Japan and the more relaxed life in Canada. I don't know if I could live in Canada all the time. I think I would miss the tight energy of Tokyo.

In 1990, when my sister and her husband bought a property on the bank of the truly majestic St. Lawrence River, it was love at first sight. I still have a strong feeling for Canada, even though I left decades ago. Canada "gave" me life and an excellent education, and I still have a sense of duty and debt. It was one of the reasons that I made a gift of my work, about five hundred paintings, drawings and prints, to the Pierre Boucher Museum in 1987. The artist in me has always felt that I should leave part of my art production to my country. I was starting to feel that I could play a more active part in the artistic life of the region.

And, of course, as an artist I would also like to be recognized in my own country. Strange, this strong impulse for an artist to be recognized. I believe that one must constantly question oneself. After ten years of trying, I don't think I will become part of the artistic world in Quebec. It's true that I am only there during the summer months, which is a quiet period in terms of exhibitions, but if I am to believe my friends, the Quebec art market is dead. No one buys anymore. In my own case, in the year 2000 I had four exhibition projects on the go in Quebec, and only one came through. Although, as I said, I see my artistic production from a very different perspective now, especially my art in relation to churches, what I call my "religious art."

This "strong impulse to be recognized"—some would call this ambition.

An artist creates to share his or her thinking, experience, emotions. He does not create for himself, even though at the moment of creation, he does not usually think of the other, the audience. The viewer will recreate the work according to his or her own experience, his own appreciation and sensibility, according to everything that forms him.

You are using the word "artist" in the larger sense, then, to refer to all arts.

Yes. Conscious of it or not, an artist is pushed by the desire to leave something to humanity. The art object he creates is like a child in the hands of a creator. This object gives him the impression that he took part in the great artistic symphony of mankind. The true artist aims at participating—by analogy, obviously—in God's creating power. He dresses himself in the Creator's vestments. He becomes a sort of shaman. The difficulty for the artist is to submit to this dimension at the same time as becoming transparent. He must let art speak for itself, even though the work has to bear the artist's mark. Transparency—Presence. Eternal dilemma and mystery of the creation of art.

In your seventieth year, after forty years of concentrated work, you were awarded a citation by the Canadian government for your artistic contribution to Japan/Canada relations. Do you have a sense of satisfaction with your artistic achievements?

Satisfaction is not the correct word. If I have had the energy to produce such a huge quantity of work, and I am not the only artist who feels this, it is because of deep "unsatisfaction" (excuse the neologism) once a work is completed. "Unsatisfaction" creates a sort of anxiety, carves a certain empty space. Anxiety about whether the work will stand, will last. Since no work is ever totally what I had in mind, what I want it to be, I am forced by an invisible pulse, a vital urge to start another work to fill up the vacant space. I could quote Alberto Giacometti who says: "Je ne sais ce que je vois qu'en travaillant"—It is only through working that I know what I see. And what I see is never exactly what I wanted to achieve.

To answer your question, I feel a certain contentment, an ease of mind, maybe, but not a satisfaction which implies a fulfilment. Otherwise, I would draw not even one more single line.

Calligraphy, 2000.

A SELECTION FROM THE WORKS OF GASTON PETIT

Faithful to the Banner (front and back). Fabric and oil on wood.

The Farm. Oil on masonite. 60x45 cm. 1960. Musée Pierre Boucher collection, Trois-Rivières, QC.

Oranges. Oil on canvas. 31.5 x 41 cm. 1987.

Fertile Eden (The Red Circle). Oil on canvas, 162 x 130 cm. 1966.

The Seasons: Spring, Summer, Fall, Winter. Fabric and oil on canvas, 4. 162 x 130 cm). 1988. Canadian Embassy collection, Tokyo, Japan.

The Family Portrait #1. Oil on canvas, 65 x 80 cm. 1971.

King David's Saga #59, Bathsheba in Her Bath. 130 x 162 cm. 1975. Ikeda 20th Century Museum of Art collection, Itoh, Japan.

Temptation of a Day. Oil on canvas, 162 x 180 cm. 1977.

One of Them. Oil on canvas, 163 x 180 cm. 1977. Private collection.

Tripod. Oil on canvas. 220 x 91 cm. 1985.

Faces of My Mother (9 out of 10). Oil on canvas, 91 x 73 cm. 1975. Bibliothèque Gabrielle Roy collection, Quebec.

Self-Portrait with Yellow Flowers. Oil on canvas, 81 x 65 cm. 1987.

The Artist By Himself. Oil on canvas, 89 x 116 cm. 1987.

The Stunning Message. Oil on fabric on wood, triptych, 200 x 280 cm. 1990. Santa Sabina collection, Rome.

O-Fukuro #98, #46, #63, #58. Paper bag collages and drawing. 1991, 1992.

Rivers of My Memory #2. Silkscreen, 85 x 55 cm. 1969.

Folds of Memory IV, VI, XIII. Felt pen on paper. 1988, 1989, 1994.

The Anvil of Forgetfulness. Woodblock, 67 x 42 cm. 1971.

Images of a Journey: Invitation, Jerusalem, Stonehenge, Ueno.
3 silkscreens and 1 lithograph, 71 x 56 cm each. 1983.

The Great Zac. Silkscreen, 80 x 56 cm. 1970.

Balzac's Family. 5 terracotta sculptures, 8-9 cm high. 1995.

Siamese. Aluminum, 42 x 49 x 25 cm. 1985.

Shiroyama Church, Nagasaki. 2000.

Seisen Chapel, Gotanda Tokyo, 1969.

Rokko Church, Kobe. 1999.